RECOMPENSE

RECOMPENSE

Streams, Summits and Reflections

Brian Irwin

Library of Congress Control Number:		2009905830
ISBN:	Hardcover	978-1-4415-4557-2
	Softcover	978-1-4415-4556-5

This book was printed in the United States of America.

Cover photo: Climbers completing the classic moderate route up *The Cosmiques Arete*,
Aguille du Midi, Chamonix, France. (Brian Irwin photo.)

Frontispiece: The Llanganuco Valley, Cordillera Blanca, Peru. (Brian Irwin photo.)

Rear cover photo: Brian Irwin. (Robert Irwin photo.)

Recompense: Streams, Summits and Reflections / Brian Irwin

Many of the selections in this book, either in part or entirety,
have been previously published:

"The Last Moonset," *Rock and Ice*, January 2007; "From Away," *The Journal of
Wilderness and Environmental Medicine*, Spring 2003; "Papa Noel," *The Journal of
Travel Medicine*, November/December 2004; "Recompense," *Alpinist*, Number 24;
"The Stalls," *Mountain Gazette*, June 2008; "Climbing Kids," *Appalachia*, Summer/
Fall 2008; "Freeski or Die: New Hampshire's Mount Washington," *Freeskier*,
January 2008; "The Cradle of American Alpinism," *Rock and Ice*, January 2010;
"Sliding on the Crown Jewel," *Powder*, October 2008; "The Beast of The East,"
Rock and Ice, July 2008; "Eastern Treat," *Couloir*, Winter 2003.

To order additional copies of this book, contact:
Xlibris Corporation
1-888-795-4274
www.Xlibris.com
Orders@Xlibris.com
62061

CONTENTS

Introduction 9

Part One: The Knife Edge

The Last Moonset 13
From Away..19
Papa Noel...26
Recompense 33
The Stalls 38
Climbing Kids...45
Koz, He's the Man...49
Floating the Swan..53

Part Two: Rime and Rocks

Freeski or Die: New Hampshire's Mount Washington 59
The Cradle of American Alpinism 71
Sliding on the Crown Jewel 81
The Beast of the East...88
Eastern Treat 99

Part Three: Running Deep

A Quality Day..107
A Bowl Full of Cherries...111
Grizzlies, Trout, and the City of Brotherly Love 118

Epilogue...129
Glossary 133
Acknowledgments...137

For Andy and Reid.

INTRODUCTION

M Y FATHER EMPHASIZED the importance of writing early in my life. Family vacations and fishing trips were exceptionally organized, with mandatory journal-writing time for the whole family inserted into the itinerary. Writing, which seemed like an onerous task early in my youth, later developed into one of the most important outlets upon which I would rely. Inking some of my most wonderful memories has not only given me the chance to perfect those recollections in my mind, but has also preserved those periods for my children to one day share. Likewise, crafting the language to express, in print, the pain of my most challenging times has given me solace and, quite often, closure. I am now at a crossroads in my life, amidst changes that have been both fantastic and difficult. This book is the culmination of a chapter of my life. I am leaving it for my friends and family to read as I look toward the future.

The selections found in this book vary widely in scope. From personal, revealing pieces to historical overviews, from nostalgic tales to impassioned recollections, many of these pieces have been published previously. However, the versions found here are the author's drafts, some of which only slightly resemble the versions that were published. Many of these selections were published in specialty magazines; however, herein all attempts were made to minimize the use of technical climbing and skiing terminology as many readers may be unfamiliar with some of the terms. In cases where such terminology was important in preserving the flavor or tone of a piece, it was left in the text; a glossary is available for these instances.

While the topics found here are broad and may seem only loosely related, the theme of the book is consistent throughout: the outdoor world and how humans interact with it yields fascinating impressions. The outdoors is a passion of mine, one I hope to share with my children throughout my life. Time spent in the mountains and streams have shaped my soul and left a spiritual mark. With the outdoors as a canvas on which to portray complex interpersonal interactions, social thought processes, and ribbons of history about our wilderness, I hope it is an enjoyable read. For you, perhaps next time you see a hillside covered in snow, a dripping cascade or a bubbling brook, you will think back to images of important people, periods, or places in your life. And perhaps, with slightly different perspective, those images will, if even just for an instant, provide you with something rich.

Brian Irwin
May 2009

Part One

The Knife Edge

Peruvian herders driving sheep toward the Ischinca Valley,
Cordillera Blanca, Peru. (Brian Irwin photo.)

THE LAST MOONSET

A S SOON AS our ski-plane landed on Alaska's Kahiltna Glacier, we ran into Ben Gilmore, a familiar face from back home in New Hampshire.

He greeted us, "Come on up and hang out. The girls just came off Mount Hunter. It's cocktail hour."

We entered Sue Nott's giant dome tent on the glacier. The huge structure, known as the Space Station, had been gifted by her sponsor, Mountain Hardwear. Piles of freeze-dried meals, ropes, and duffels were sprinkled around the edges of the enormous structure. Everyone was sitting comfortably on foam pads. Sue lounged in her pink jacket next to her friend Zoe Hart, sipping cherry Kool-Aid and vodka, recalling their attempt of the classic alpine climb known as *Deprivation*.

"Send it! Arrrghh!" Zoe mock-screamed at her as she took a sip of the ratty cocktail. "Remember that?" Sue laughed, then turned and asked me if I'd ever hung out before in Talkeetna, the town from which we departed. I hadn't.

"Just wait until you get back there and spend a day or two. The only thing more interesting than climbing in Alaska is meeting the locals! You're going to love it," she said. We sipped whiskey and listened to Ozzy tunes for hours with Ben, Zoe, Sue and John Varco, who was her boyfriend at the time. Sue told me about her near-death accident on one of Vail's mixed routes during which her abdomen was impaled by a fallen ice pillar. I didn't know Sue; I had only met her twice. I was riveted by her stories. She was very energetic and unbelievably excited. Her partner,

Karen McNeill, was due to arrive in a few days to join her on an attempt on Mount Foraker's the *Infinite Spur*.

Kahiltna Glacier airstrip, Alaska. (Brian Irwin photo.)

Two weeks later, my partner Eric and I returned from Denali's fourteen-thousand-foot camp after a failed attempt on *Thunder Ridge*. Sue and Karen had left the day before for their climb. We pulled our cache from Sue's tent and left her a thank-you note. Our plans to climb the Mini-Moonflower Buttress during our last day on the glacier were stymied by a flurry of seracs that persistently calved off Mount Hunter, pounding the valley below. One enormous slide had brushed Ben and his partner as they scouted Hunter's North Ridge. Instead, we settled for a short route on Mount Frances on which we had our own heels dusted by an avalanche and flew back to Talkeetna.

After the requisite shower at the bunkhouse and burger at the West Rib Bar, we headed to the town park on the shores of the Talkeetna River. It was 10:00 p.m., and the sky was as bright as day. Walking by a group huddled on a giant log beside a campfire, I heard a voice.

"Don't be shy," an old woman said to me from her perch on the log. She winked once and took a pull from a bottle of wine. "My name is Fern. Come on over and join us." I walked over. Fern passed me her wine. I took a sip and gave it back.

"Nice here, isn't it?" Fern asked.

The Moonflower Buttress of Mount Hunter, Alaska. This serac avalanche dropped over a vertical mile onto the glacier below, barely sparing the lives of Ben Gilmore and partner. (Brian Irwin photo.)

"Yes," I replied, looking at the horizon. The sun cast orange light across the giant peaks on the skyline.

By midnight no one was sober. "One Tooth Guy" was quibbling with Shannon, a loud, obnoxious musher who was calling him the "ugliest piece of shit I've ever seen." Tauras the Guitarist, recognizable in similar forms across the country as the eccentric, outspoken political activist frequently seen in the city parks, strumming away as he stands alone, breaking strings left and right. I asked him to play some Ben Harper.

Tauras said loudly, "I don't have any of that, but how about some Byrds?" He leaned in and whispered, "I can't really play the guitar. I just strum and sing the lyrics, but no one notices. It gets me ass." Meat, the co-owner of a Talkeetna motel, heaved a log the length of his F-250 into the fire, stood on the flaming log, held up his beer, and screamed, "I'm one-quarter Athabascan!" His girlfriend stood next to me, wearing a tight camouflage T-shirt that read "Pornstar" in glitter paint across her chest.

After Meat's ancestral proclamation, she punched my arm and yelled into my face, "He really is, you know. You better respect it."

"Respect what?" I asked.

Pornstar rolled her eyes. "Athabascan. You know, we're all descendants of the Athabascan. Even Jesus was."

Fern, whom I hadn't seen since she invited us into the party, walked up with a plastic bag and pulled out a dead trout the length of my arm, saying, "Larry caught it for me."

"I'd love to catch one of those!" I said.

"Larry!" she screamed. "Take this boy fishing!"

Larry was the son of a famous Alaskan bush pilot, but he turned out a bit more peculiar than his charismatic father. He had a flat, medicated affect and an odd facial tick that rang of instability. Larry sped over from the other side of the fire on his ATV, clinching a basset hound puppy by the neck as he rounded the giant log. He grabbed my arm, pulled me aboard, and sped down the riverbank to his fishing hole. We didn't catch any fish; and his dog, Hershey Bar, fell in the icy river twice.

Around 3:00 a.m., the town's kindergarten teacher jumped on a log and yelled, "It's happening!" Everyone by the fire cheered and ran down river. We followed. The gang stopped in a clearing and stared into the southwestern sky. The moon was enormous, a rich amber hue, hung up in the trees south of town. Everyone stood in silence, even Meat, as the moon sank below the horizon for the last time this spring. It wouldn't rise again until autumn.

Eric Seifer on *Thunder Ridge*, Denali, Alaska. (Brian Irwin photo.)

We stayed by the river until sunrise. As the outline of the Alaska Range emerged on the horizon, I stared at Mount Foraker. It was Sue and Karen's third day on the *Infinite Spur*. My eyes shifted to Denali. A lenticular cloud was building over its summit. In the days to come, a storm packed with hurricane-force winds would envelop the range.

A week later I was back at work. I got a call from a friend who climbs with Varco. He told me that Sue and Karen were missing on Mount Foraker, having never emerged from that huge storm.

I scrambled to contact friends from Denali's National Park Service patrol, guides and local climbers, trying to find out what happened. I read about the discovery of boot tracks high on Foraker and the recovery of a pack from the base of the route. The belief that the women surmounted the technical section of their route but were hit just below the summit by winds estimated to be in excess of one hundred miles per hour. Over the next week, I followed the ongoing search very closely. The more I dug for new information or promising findings, the more I realized that although there were theories, this incident was a mystery; and tragically, it may always remain one.

After the trip, I was back at work, sitting at my tiny desk, my mind drifting between idyllic memories of my expedition and images of Sue's pink jacket. Occasionally I'd stumble onto a Web site that had a photo of Sue, grinning widely, wearing her pink jacket or an aerial photo that showed that same jacket atop an avalanche debris pile at the base of the *Infinite Spur*. Every time I saw a photo of that jacket, I felt a lump in my throat. I remember telling Sue that night in her giant tent that it was a garment of which my sister would be jealous. I couldn't get it out of my mind.

I vividly recalled the sensation of my pulse in my temples as we plodded up the glacier. The sensation of swinging into Denali's cold, brittle ice. The deafening roar and bitter aerosolized, snow-filled wind gusts of Hunter's avalanches that poured up and over the mountain known as Radio Control Tower. And the charm of Sue Nott's giggle over a Kool-Aid cocktail as she relaxed against a bright orange tent wall while the sun slipped behind the ridgeline and the coldness of the mountains rose from the valley.

FROM AWAY

CLIMBERS FROM THE Western United States are incredulous when they hear a description of Maine's Mount Katahdin. Certainly, few Washington or Colorado residents, who have fourteen-thousand-foot peaks in their backyards, would regard this bump to be a worthy, formidable mountaineering objective. Mount Katahdin is a loose primarily basalt and granite peak that Mainers—and Maine transplants deservingly referred to as "from away"—hold proudly as the crown jewel of Baxter State Park.

Katahdin appears transplanted from the Rockies; it has multiple summits linked by over two thousand feet of sheer cliffs that hold some of the East's most committing remote rock climbs. The cliff faces climb steeply to a six-inch-wide, one-mile-long "Knife Edge," perhaps the single most thrilling stretch of hiking trail in New England.

The enormous park is pure wilderness and well preserved. It's roughly two hundred thousand acres of thick pine forests, trout-filled alpine tarns, and lichen-covered granite boulders left behind as the glaciers that covered this entire area receded many thousand of years ago. Most of the huge boulder fields have filled in their clefts with forests of stunted trees, termed Krummholtz, near the timberlines and are unrecognizable as glacial ridges or moraines.

One Sunday night during my residency, I was on call for my typical twenty-four-hour shift on the maternity ward. One woman in labor and another with serious complications leading to a 3:00 a.m. Cesarean section kept me busy all night. Monday morning the action was over, and I was heading out, looking forward to two days off. I'd thought about climbing Katahdin, but a storm forecast shifted plans toward paddling the Sandy River instead. Stuffing my stethoscope into my bag as I entered the stairwell, I heard a patient declare, "Dr. Irwin, my water broke!" I turned to see my young patient in a wheelchair with an ear-to-ear smile and outstretched arms. "You're staying to deliver me, aren't you?"

Rime ice on Katahdin's Knife Edge. (Brian Irwin photo.)

Based on her exam, I thought surely she'd deliver by noon, and my day off would be salvaged. However, she had a difficult labor. And it wasn't until 7:30 that evening that I made it home. Immediately after I collapsed on my couch, my pager went off. Instead of a hospital number, the device displayed a complex dispatch code, engineered by the Wilderness Rescue Team (WRT), for which I volunteered. A technical rescue was in place on Mount Katahdin. Exhausted, I packed up and headed out.

I thought joining the WRT would be a great way to "blow off steam" during residency. At this point, the intelligence of this decision was in doubt since there was no steam left to blow. Regardless, I'd been conscripted—by my own doing. I drove three hours to the park's gate, picked up the dispatcher's instructions and radio at the gate, and hiked the three miles by headlamp, my light boring a tunnel through humid air under threatening skies.

At 2:30 a.m., I met the other rescuers at Chimney Pond's backcountry ranger cabin. The floor was cluttered with ropes, carabiners, and pulleys piled among headlamps, a folding litter, and splints. The ranger briefed us.

Lincoln McNulty and Marta Boyd, two experienced climbers, had topped out on the *Armadillo* (5.7, IV),* Mount Katahdin's showpiece alpine rock climb. McNulty rappelled off to retrieve a stuck piece of protection, but out of exhaustion, he had failed to properly thread his rope through the anchor. He fell, taking the rope with him as he tumbled onto a brushy ledge. With no way to rappel, Boyd had climbed down to McNulty where together they tried to descend to the base of the cliff despite McNulty's injuries. Unfortunately, their rope became stuck. They abandoned it, and the two resigned themselves to hunkering down on an exposed ledge with six hundred feet of technical terrain above them and a thousand more below.

Conrad Yager climbing Katahdin's *Pamola IV* (5.6, IV). (Brian Irwin photo.)

---

* Rock climbs in the United States are rated using the Yosemite Decimal System. Fourth-class climbs rarely require a rope. Fifth-class climbs require a rope and are rated from 5.0 (easiest) to 5.15 (hardest). The grade or commitment level of a route is rated from I (least committing in terms of time and exposure) to VI (a very committing multiday climb).

The rescue leader dictated that all rescuers would scramble 1,200 feet to the base of the cliffs. From there, three rope teams would lead up to the victims, administer first aid, and lower them in litters hundreds of feet down to the less steep mountainside below. There a National Guard helicopter would extricate them to the closest trauma center in Bangor, Maine. With the support of the ten other rescuers, two three-man rope teams spent an hour and a half approaching the cliffs from the cabin. The rock face loomed over Chimney Pond. The cabin and a few lean-tos were cluttered on the eastern shore of the pond. We carefully hopped rocks along the dark, rippling shore to the far side where we followed the streambed that fed the pond. The boulders were slick with wet lichen. More than one rescuer plunged a foot into the frigid pools of bubbling water after slipping and losing balance due to the awkward weight of a shifting backpack full of rescue gear.

Climbing the last few hundred yards before the cliff band was an eerie, surreal experience. No one was talking. The only sound I heard through the wind was my own deep breathing and the bounding thump of my pulse in my temples. My headlamp cast a cone-shaped beam through the steam of my breath onto a huge clearing of leveled trees, all dead, all pointing downhill.

They were battered and weathered, much like the driftwood you would find on the wild coast of Washington State. Some were still loosely connected to their intact stumps by stringy bands of wood that were shattered as the avalanche that ran through this area caused their trunks to explode and splinter in all directions.

At the bottom of the cliff band, we organized gear. I was climbing with my pack, heavy with medication, airways, splints, and IVs. A twenty-pound folding litter was lashed to my pack. No matter how I arranged this four-foot-long tube, it was difficult to manage. Either it swung down and hit my calves or it stuck out wide like a burdensome log resting on my shoulders.

Up we climbed, first on a friction slab, and then working left onto a ledge for a horrendous four-hundred-foot traverse through gnarled, sharp, and growth-stunted shrubbery. Dawn was not far off, so climbing this ledge, I could make out the silhouettes of the angry thick branches in the dense thicket we penetrated. The wind was picking up considerably and had shifted to the east during the last hour. Low-lying clouds heaved up and over the Knife Edge, pouring onto us and occasionally robbing our view of the lantern in the ranger cabin's window far below. As the sky brightened a little, one could make out the bubbling cauldron-like underside of the enormous cumulonimbus cloud that was overhead.

We clambered up many more terraced faces and, finally, up a long rock rib to the victims' ledge. The two rangers on the first rope team were tending to the victims. We gingerly traversed the narrow ledge, crossing slick rock and two small cascades. The victims were huddled behind a short windbreak they had made. Boyd was crouching; Lincoln was lying in a Mylar bivy sack on top of a foam pad. He had fallen on his leg and shoulder before his ear and jaw finally brought him to a halt against a rock.

Boyd was worried about Lincoln's mental state.

"He's been saying weird stuff all night. He's confused. He's been passing out on and off. His ear's hurt real bad, but it's not bleeding. It does have some clear fluid coming out of it, though."

Based on the height of the fall and severity of injuries, we knew we'd need a helicopter; however, the landing zone was far below us, at the floor of the cirque. To get the patient to that part of the basin, we would have to lower him almost six hundred feet down seventy-degree slabs, a technical, risky, and time-consuming process. This information was radioed to the crew aboard the Black Hawk helicopter that had been dispatched from the National Guard and had been circling the basin for the previous hour.

Helicopter rescues are rare in the Eastern United States. They are much more common in Europe, like this rescue of a climber with a fractured femur from high on the *Hornli Ridge*, the Matterhorn, Switzerland. (Brian Irwin photo.)

The helicopter crew decided to attempt a pick-off from the ledge. The wind was blowing into the basin at thirty miles per hour, with frequent stronger gusts, and was pushing the chopper into the mountain. The helicopter rose very slowly, constantly making fine adjustments to counter the wind. Initially below us, it rose to our level within minutes, at one point hovering just a few hundred feet off the cliff. We could see eye to eye with the pilot. He inched toward and over us, easing into the granite wall. There was no margin of error as he navigated through the cold rain that fell in fierce sheets against our efforts.

Chimney Pond in Katahdin's South Basin. (Brian Irwin photo.)

A medic was lowered, and Lincoln was neatly packaged.

"Dis ith cool!" he screamed over the noise of the helicopter.

"Wait till you get the bill!" I yelled back.

The cable was clipped, the safety line attached, and Lincoln was promptly hoisted inside the chopper. I rappelled down with his climbing partner, slowly and not so eloquently. At the bottom, scores of rescuers took our bags and the unopened litter. Alone, I sloshed through the streambed down to Chimney Pond, ate a sandwich, and began the hike out at 11:00 a.m.

As I arrived at the trailhead, thunder clapped once, and the sky opened up. As I paused to rest at the trailhead, a well-dressed newscaster in high heels slid out from behind a big oak and thrust an oversized foam-covered microphone into my face. I answered a few of her questions. Later, when I saw the edited news clip, I barely recognized myself as the filthy sleep-deprived guy who babbled incessantly about "rocks wet, things hard, fast wind . . ."

The next week, I went to get a haircut at the tiny Norman Rockwellesque barbershop in my small Maine town. Dusty bottles of yellow elixirs and tarnished brass-handled shaving mugs rested on a shallow crooked shelf just behind the door. The barber started to cut my hair and then stopped. He pushed his narrow black plastic-rimmed glasses up from the end of his nose, pulled his head back, and stared me in the face. Quickly he directed his eyes down at his maroon nylon overshirt and started brushing off hair clippings. Without looking up he asked, "Aren't you that guy?"

"Which guy?" I asked. He stopped brushing and looked up at me.

"You know, that guy up there a couple of nights ago. Up north."

"You mean Baxter?" I confirmed.

"Yeah, that guy. The news said they just let him out of the hospital." He started brushing his shirt again.

"I heard that," I answered.

He pulled back, deposing me with a critical look.

"You grow up here?"

"No. I grew up in Maryland. I'm here for work," I sheepishly replied.

He pulled his glasses back down to the end of his nose and again started to cut.

"Don't matta any. That guy was one lucky bastard. And you mighta done good, son, but you're still from away."

Papa Noel

ROUGH HANDS SCRAPED the nylon wall next to my head. I awoke to a soft voice whispering, "Doctor! Doctor! Mi nina esta infermo! Por favor, doctor!"

I rose from my sleeping bag and unzipped the tent door. A full moon illuminated a woman holding her child. The dramatic peaks of the Bolivian Andes glowed behind her, towering over our base camp. The mother wore a tattered dress layered with sweaters and shawls. She held a brightly colored handmade sling in which lay a sick girl. My headlamp shone across the child's face, revealing weathered, sun-damaged cheeks and a runny nose. The child stared blankly at the sky. Occasionally a raspy cough shook her body and showed strain across her face. She was not crying.

Condoriri base camp. (Brian Irwin photo.)

We had few medications in our expedition's first aid kit, but we did have some old antibiotics. As I fidgeted in the dark with the tablets and a Swiss Army knife, the child had an intense coughing fit that lasted a few minutes. By the time the toxic-appearing girl caught her breath, I could clearly see that her lips, though sun scorched and dry, were clearly blue.

Eight days before in a hotel in the capital city of La Paz, we spent the morning drinking fresh coffee and asking for seconds on omelets. We showered, got dressed, and checked out of our rooms. Our outfitter carried all our bags; custom dictates that loading your own gear is rude and implies that one's "staff" is weak. So we watched, lazily, as our porters lashed duffels of expensive gear and crates of food onto the top of three Toyota Land Cruisers. On the way out of La Paz, we napped behind $100 sunglasses and listened to personal CD players. Occasionally we would stop and take out our pricy digital cameras to photograph the dramatic scenery. A colorful marketplace. A woman washing clothes in a river. Children playing soccer.

Children and their mothers wait for the doctor in the school courtyard, Chunavi, Bolivia. (Brian Irwin photo.)

The dusty road to base camp winds across the bone-dry Altiplano. On the horizon are the magnificent peaks of Bolivia's Cordillera Real, our climbing objective. Over twenty thousand feet in elevation, their granite shoulders are draped with hanging blue glaciers, leaking fine ribbons of meltwater from their snouts. The only settlement on this route is the small village of Chunavi. It is a cold, sad town with not a tree in sight to protect it from the howling winds that scour the plains on their way to the Andes. There are no phones. No marketplace. No doctors.

We pulled off the dusty road, down an alley between two rows of crumbling adobe homes. In the schoolyard, patients were already waiting. No men were present, only women and children. The women were dressed in ornate, colorful, traditional garb. They talked, breastfed, or spun alpaca yarn while they were waiting for the clinic to start. Out of the school, which had been closed this week to allow its use as a medical clinic, came the village mayor. His face was badly scarred. He smiled and shook my hand. He spoke to me in Quecha, a pre-Inca language, which I did not understand.

A high adobe wall surrounded the schoolyard. A few blocks were missing, leaving a hole. Through the hole, I saw a group of men walking across the adjacent field and toward the school. "The village leaders," Carlos, my Bolivian contact, whispered to me. They entered the schoolyard and surrounded me. Suspiciously, and through two translators, the mayor spoke.

High on Bolivia's Nevado Illimani. (Brian Irwin photo.)

"What do you want from our village? Why do you want to help us? What do you want in return?"

At first I was surprised. I expected a warm welcome, not skepticism. Then, I glanced across the courtyard at our three shiny SUVs, loaded high with gear and food. I looked at the work-hardened faces of the men who surrounded me. I looked down at my boots. I was embarrassed.

"This is your land. These are your mountains. We climb here. You live here. We are your guests and would like to offer a gift. We bring a doctor, a nurse, and enough medicine to treat your village." The men mumbled, exchanged looks, and broke out in laughter. They closed in on me and ruffled my hair. The mayor raised a steer horn and pressed it to his lips. He blew it into the sky. Within fifteen minutes there were three hundred people in the schoolyard, playing ball, chatting, waiting to see the doctor.

Chunavi's village leaders inquire about our intentions, Chunavi, Bolivia. (Photo from Brian Irwin collection.)

The school was one room. It held two handcrafted benches and a table. The walls were adobe, and the roof was thatched with reed.

Carlos's nephew, a neurologist from La Paz, was helping us with the clinic and translating. The two of us worked while giggling children kicked balls and drew with crayons in the courtyard. The "triage table" was littered with stickers and candy brought by our team.

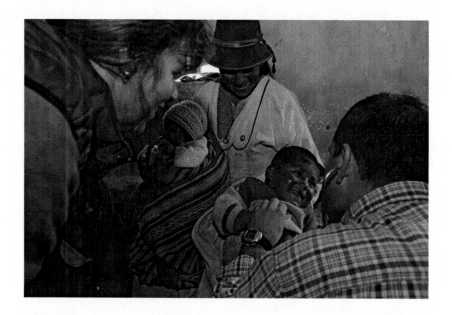

Young boy with solar dermatitis, a harmless condition whereby one's cheeks become darkened as a result of prolonged exposure to intense UV radiation, as often occurs at high altitude. (Photo from Brian Irwin collection.)

Within a week we treated the entire town. Parasitic infections. Pregnancy. Fungal infections. Tuberculosis. Low back pain. Some things we could treat. Others we couldn't. It was frustrating. As doctors, we want to heal. We want to cure, but sometimes all we can do is examine and listen. Often, pain control was all we could offer, and this was understood. The townspeople were incredibly grateful, hugging and thanking us, asking when we would return.

Before we departed, the mayor and his advisors again circled me in the courtyard. They presented me with an ornately decorated notarized letter from the Government of Chunavi, thanking us for our help. Translated, the letter read, "Your gift was like that brought to the children on Christmas. We feel like we have been visited by *Papa Noel*." As we loaded into our trucks, a man, Jose, approached me. He had walked six hours through the night from his isolated farm to ask for our help. He urged me to visit his wife before I left. She was too ill to come to the schoolyard. She had been sick for a year and had never seen a doctor.

We drove across the plains for an hour to Jose's one-room home. We entered, walking past a rusty, tireless bicycle, a hitching post, and a mule. In the corner of the room, there was a tattered single mattress. Jose's six family members shared this bed. It had no sheets. On the bed was a woman, lying perfectly still, wrapped in soiled shawls and blankets. She made eye contact with me and then looked away. I approached her and eased onto the corner of the bed; the mattress shifted, moving the woman very slightly. She wailed in pain for an instant. A tear streamed down her cheek. Her husband dashed to her side. Through translators, in Quecha, he told me, "She went blind a year ago. Her arms and legs hurt so badly she can't move them. She has trouble breathing, and she won't eat. And then this happened . . ." He unwrapped her dry, cracked hands to reveal them. Her fingers were severely subluxed, characteristic of rheumatoid arthritis. As I gave her steroids and explained her disease to her, a gust of cold wind sliced through the house and rattled the uninsulated tin roof over the woman's bed.

After the clinic, we sent all leftover medications back to La Paz to be donated to a hospital. I hadn't anticipated a woman bringing a one-year-old girl with pneumonia ten miles up the trail on a mule, through the night, to seek the help of the nearest doctor. Feverishly I crushed tablets and stirred Gatorade mix to create a makeshift antibiotic suspension. We force-fed it to the child, gave a Ziploc bag of the concoction to the patient's mother, and crossed our fingers. The child stayed overnight at camp and was taken on mule back to town in the morning. A week later the mother reappeared to our base camp, in the afternoon this time, with the girl in her arms. She approached me and held out her child. The young girl smiled and giggled.

Paul Cormier leading Pequenyo Alpamayo, Cordillera Real, Bolivia. (Brian Irwin photo.)

We plodded up the glacier as the sun rose over the Amazon basin far to the east. It flicked orange light onto the summit of the peak across the valley. In the crisp morning air, I could see each breath as I heard the metronome of my pulse deep inside my ears. I thought of the people in the Altiplano, already working in their fields. I pictured a sick woman on a bed. A rusty, tireless bicycle. A little girl with blue lips. As I looked at my feet, warm inside my expensive mountaineering boots, I felt ashamed. And I thought about Papa Noel.

RECOMPENSE

*M*Y *GREASY PALMS clasped the granite ledge, damp from the humid New Hampshire air. As I carefully mantled up and onto my feet, I felt the exposure as I noticed the tiny trees below, somehow thriving on the steep slope littered with boulders. That same move always made me nervous; but once stable, I rested on the platform, my pulse rate falling. Observations of the rock's gristly texture and the vertiginous sensation of the route toggled back and forth in my mind with images of Rand's medical record, its pages flipping for a hint of a mistake I'd made or a clue I'd missed. I didn't find any of that. Rand didn't warn the world or his doctors of his plans. He just followed through with them. He hid his feelings well. Well enough to surprise everyone who knew him when he took his life on September 2, 2007.*

Recompense is a striking route. It starts with a series of overlaps and corners and ends in a brilliant corner. Only the dirty chimney on the second pitch detracts from the climb's aesthetics. Most people bypass that pitch, avoiding the unpleasant, imperfect nature of the rock by choosing a more defined parallel flake. It's a fractured route because of this inconsistency, which is fitting because it was on this route that Rand fell in 2003 and shattered his ankle. Ironically, it was this incident that introduced him to a number of people in the climbing community, including Rick Wilcox, owner of International Mountain Equipment in North Conway, New Hampshire, who became his future employer.

I met Rand years earlier on a brittle day in late October.

"His name is Rand McNally? You've got to be kidding me! Is he related to that map guy?" I asked Eric as he pointed to the man skiing

33

effortlessly uphill toward us. Steam floated off the skin-tight polypro that encased his fit upper body like shrink-wrap.

"I don't think so, at least not directly. He's a great guy. You guys have a lot in common. He's a commercial airline pilot . . ."

"I'm not an airline pilot," I replied.

"I know. Stop interrupting. He's a doctor too. You'll like skiing with him."

It was the first day Bretton Woods Ski Area was blowing snow, and everyone was anxious to ski. Lifts wouldn't open for weeks, early season ice climbs hadn't yet formed, and the rock was too cold to climb. In New England, where our "good" conditions pound the hell out of ski bases, locals don't think twice about carving up a little turf and kicking off a few sparks from exposed rocks in order to make a half-dozen turns on man-made névé.

"Come on, slowpokes!" Rand hollered to me as I lagged behind. "Just because I don't know you doesn't mean I can't race you!"

I'd just met him, but I flipped him off anyway. He smiled, smeared his glove across his glistening generous forehead, whipped his neck, snapping flecks of perspiration off the frosty tips of his salt-and-pepper hair, and laughed in a soft, charming tone.

We quickly became friends. He chose me as his doctor, a fact that he did not hide and often gave me permission to mention freely. Doctoring another doctor is a unique experience, an honor really, but also complicated and challenging. Appointments were full of jokes yet were productive and focused. He'd come clean with me, or so I thought, much more so than other patient-friends of mine do during their checkups. He was an outgoing guy, social and resourceful.

Reaching for the next move, I pressed my ear against the wide crack as I thrust my arm deep inside, blindly scratching for a positive feature. The hollow gash in the rock's face hummed with eerie energy. In my mind I could picture that smile and hear Rand's sharp cackle from deep inside the chasm as if it were ricocheting off the walls of my exam room. I missed it.

In a matter of weeks after meeting him, Rand had me calling his lab results to his place of work, International Mountain Equipment, and sometimes even dropping off his prescriptions there. I didn't mind. Errands like that often turned into cups of coffee or laps on short local after-work rock climbs. Approach and belay-ledge conversations between us rattled with raucous jokes and hilarious stories.

Although he'd done very well in medical school, Rand had chosen not to practice, instead pursuing a career in the navy and later as an airline pilot. He'd raised a family and eventually moved to the valley, semiretired at a fairly young age. But he still found creative uses for his medical degree. He'd occasionally call my office and notify the staff that Dr. McNally was on the phone with an important question for Dr. Irwin. My nurse would dash down to my exam room, interrupt me, and advise me of "a call from another doctor on line 3." When I'd pick up, it'd be Rand, asking me to climb or hike. It was a pain in the ass. But I kind of liked it. It was fun, like Rand.

I torqued my fingers into the damp slot, moved up a few feet to a stable stance, and rested. It was strange knowing Rand once stood on this very terrace. The rock was slick, much like it was on the humid day Rand fell on this same pitch. I tried to focus as I nervously smeared on the balls of my feet. But dialogue invaded my brain. I remembered an early conversation with Rand.

"Where'd you go to medical school?" I once asked him.

"Texas. While I was living there, I heard a rumor that medical school was cheap if you were a resident and that application numbers were down. I thought, what the hell . . ."

My foot slipped from the ledge. I scrambled to regain a stable stance, clinging to talc-caked crystals with my fingertips. My daydream screeched to a halt as I scrambled to reorient myself to reality not memory. I pulled my feet under me; thoughts of our discussion immediately restarted.

"I thought it'd be neat, and an MD is always something nice to have in your back pocket."

"Back pocket?" I'd said sarcastically and maybe a little jealously. "All that's in my back pocket is a wad of student loan statements."

He chuckled sympathetically. It was difficult to imagine Rand needing anything in his back pocket. He put so much energy into his family, his climbing, his friends, and his passions. He was one of those guys who simply pissed you off because he was good at everything he did.

I discharged a cam into the crack and clipped it. Relieved, I let my mind wander for a moment, searching for some sense of closure from touching the same coarse minerals that Rand once did. I nearly fell as another fragment of our talks returned with haunting force.

"Brian, you're a doctor," Rand casually said. "What does someone who's a doctor do if they don't want to be a doctor and they just want to be outside as much as possible?"

At the time, I remember being both amused and confused. Rand seemed so organized. So happy. So together. He was multifaceted and bright. How could he lack focus? I know now that he was lost, more lost than anyone suspected. He hid his lack of focus or desperation behind a curtain of charisma, energy, and a fun-loving demeanor.

Doctors are hardwired to think and operate in a certain methodical way. While climbing with Rand, one part of my brain would quiver with electricity as I fiddled with a stopper while a deeper center would slowly idle, efficiently processing the guts and core of everything he said. As he would incessantly chatter on the ledge below, I imagine Rand's brain was doing the same thing. We were both processing different questions, mine being the integrity of the flake on which I was hanging, Rand's being something I'll never know, the answers to which we needed to find in order to live through that moment. Nothing drives a doctor crazier than not finding the answer. It's what we live to do.

Medicine, health, the mind, and the earth are very illusionary. They seem tangible and explainable, but often they are not. It's frustratingly often that we don't find an answer to our questions. But if we struggle through that period in time, over that broken chasm of darkness and mystery, we survive to search for the answer another day or perhaps accept the unknown and move on to the next question. Rand paid the ultimate price in an attempt to find the answer to his question. I'll never know what question to which Rand couldn't find the answer, nor will I ever know if I, or if anyone, could have thrown him a line to pull him across the darkness. But in my mind I keep traversing that hole, that bottomless shaft, looking for the light at its bottom. I make the move to the other side, successfully each time, but still living, like all of Rand's friends and family, in wonder.

I finally swung my leg up and onto the top of Recompense, clipping in and signaling to my partner below with a sharp shout. As my harness sank into my sweaty thighs, I looked back down the last pitch, which drops off into a dark, dirty chimney, and to Echo Lake where Rand's memorial service had been held just weeks earlier.

During the service I stood behind a tree, hood up and wearing sunglasses. Fat raindrops drummed the top of my hood and rolled forward, dripping off and into the muddy puddle at my feet. Across

Echo Lake, curtains of rain fell in gentle sheets onto the looming face of Cathedral Ledge.

Rand's son Neal spoke, under the tent in the pouring rain, about his father. He stood tall, inadvertently leaning the same way his father did and with the same robust confidence. He spoke about how he missed his dad but was doing well and was looking forward to fresh turns with his dad in the afterlife.

"I miss you, Dad. But I'll see you soon. Someday we'll be out of the White Mountains, together in heaven, again raising heel in knee-deep powder."

The words sliced my throat like razor blades as I tried to prevent myself from bursting into tears. I spun around, out of embarrassment, flinging water off my visor, and faced the lake. A breeze floated another veil of mist against Cathedral's the *Prow*. A thin ribbon of water ran down the dihedral to its right and dripped, swiftly and smoothly, over the broken but beautiful ledges of *Recompense*.

The Stalls

"CLOSE THE DOOR, gringo!" Emelio shouted as the door to the Patagonian refugio burst open. Curtains flipped up and over their rods, my water bottle blew over, and the Italians shifted silently on the beechwood benches, looking at each other until Jon swung the door shut, sealing out the valley's incessant winds.

As I shifted my ass on the bench, Jon flipped out the screen on his camcorder. Its speaker spewed the relentless scream of air blowing off the Hielo Sur. The video was a self-documentary of Jon, windblown and battered, trying to hike uphill but getting blown backward with inflated cheeks as his shirt snapped in the wind.

"The worst part is the haul bag is missing."

Poincenot and the Fitz Roy group, Argentine Patagonia. (Brian Irwin photo.)

I was depressed and tired of wondering what happened to our cache. We'd been waiting for over a week at base camp in the Rio Electrico Valley, waiting for stable climbing weather. This is a pastime in Patagonia; often, it's the only thing expeditions to this corner of Argentina do. Slackline walking, card playing, and heavy drinking are all important skills to have at any Patagonian base camp; and regardless of your luck with the region's notoriously infrequent and short weather windows, you'll come home better at all of them.

Pressed up against Piedra del Fraile, the enormous glacial erratic for which our campground was named, was a row of open, now-retired horse stalls. The dilapidated structures were being used as cooking and organizational space for anxious climbing teams at Fraile, all of whom hoped for stable skies. As I dashed from the refugio toward my stall, cold wind-driven water bounced off my eyes. The imposing granite spires, Mermoz and Aguja Guillamet, loomed over the wind-torn trees. Hurricane-speed winds pressed against their sturdy branches as they fought to stay upright.

I sat on a mule bag, drinking coffee diluted by the rain leaking through the stall's roof. I stared as flecks of dirt circled the surface of my pale drink. A tattered coil of retired rope lay submerged in a puddle in the courtyard, its lasso shape preserved in caked mud.

"You guys from the states?" Emelio said as he leaned over the stall's wall. "What are you cooking? Why do you have so much cheese?"

We'd met Emelio and his family the night before over cups of maté tea. They were locals who hiked into the valley for a weekend camping trip. He leaned back against the face of the huge boulder, pulled out a joint, and lit it. Smoke rolled across his face, tangling in his beard as it cartwheeled and drifted into our stall. He glanced at his wife, who carefully wiped her fingers dry in her cleavage prior to accepting his pass. She took a drag and looked at me.

"Fumada?"

Her sons ran shirtless in the dark night, jumping in puddles as everyone else at Fraile slept. I caught a glimpse of the delighted kids in soaked cotton and wool clothes as they dashed past our stall. I adjusted the pit zips on my jacket. I looked over at my thousand-dollar rack and overpriced tent and down at my Gore-Tex shoes. I was embarrassed. The stove sputtered as it ran out of gas, laughing at me as it crashed. The only happy people in Fraile that night were Emelio and his kids.

When I opened my eyes in the morning, the glow of the tent's green fabric meant one thing: sunny weather. I dragged my earplugs out of my ears. When they popped free, the silence was shattered by what sounded like an airplane taking off from my vestibule. We weren't climbing today. We weren't even going up to look for our gear.

The courtyard at Friale. (Brian Irwin photo.)

The courtyard in front of the stalls was protected from the wind. Patagonian flora and fauna are unique and diverse. The week prior, I saw a green parrot land on my tent. Now, a week later, I stared at the flowerbed, impressed as I watched bright blue orchids surprise me as I noticed them waving in the wind, taunting the unprotected and battered Lenga trees on the other side of the stream. The puddles were dry; the ropes now swung coiled in the filthy hands of Rodrigo's sons as they played gaucho. Rodrigo owned the property at Friale and was a year-round gaucho, or cowboy. His boys grew up in the shadow of these great peaks and played hide-and-seek daily with some of the world's best alpinists. Yet they wanted to grow up to be something better, just like their dad.

"Papa, Rico es mal!" echoed across the courtyard.

Emelio's boys pushed each other, fighting over whose turn it was to ride "the Bull," a rusty fifty-five-gallon drum suspended from old rope between two trees. Rodrigo's eldest lassoed both of them. They all burst into laughter and ran off toward the stalls.

Emelio's and Rodrigo's children go to school together. Emelio visits Fraile often. Although Rodrigo doesn't speak a word of English, Emelio does, and he and I talked quite a bit during the week. Over maté one afternoon, drifting in and out of "Spanglish," I picked his mind, curious to hear what a local has to say about living in the most idyllic mountain town in the world, one that is on the verge of ruin from overdevelopment.

Playing "gaucho" at Friale, Argentina. (Brian Irwin photo.)

"You must love living in Chalten, eh?"

"It's OK, but different now. Too much money coming in, not enough money staying. The people who visit are nice, but they have everything. And they come here, wait for weeks, and try to lay claim to Cerro Torre too. Then what?" he asked.

"I don't want to climb the Torre," I said defensively, realizing that I probably couldn't succeed at scaling perhaps the most notoriously insurmountable finger of rock in the world.

"It's just too much . . . how do you say . . . hype. Everyone wants to be famous. To look famous," Emelio continued.

"I just want to have fun," I replied. "That's why I climb."

"Are you having fun waiting . . . ?" His words were cut short as his giggling children tackled his legs. He darted off, chasing them with his arms in the air.

The famous Italian climbing club, the Lycos Spiders, hadn't left the refugio's table all week, except for the occasional lap up the training structure that hung from a tee in the courtyard, referred to by alpinists as a Bacher ladder. They too moped around, occasionally arguing with each other, but for the most part sitting silently and reading. I watched their matching red warm-up outfits shifting through the scratched window of the refugio as I sat on a rock rereading *Hills Like White Elephants*. My feet ached as they dangled in the roiling eddies of the milky Rio Electrico.

The Lycos Spiders' cooking stall at Piedra Fraile, Argentine Patagonia. (Brian Irwin photo.)

That night, back at the stalls, the festering continued. Jon shivered after he took a sip of the cheap liquor, exhaling forcefully to blow the rancid vapor out of his nose. "That stuff is disgusting!" he screamed, his voice echoing through the broken-down structures. He passed me the cup.

A smashed, empty plastic whisky bottle floated in the puddle to my right. A thin meniscus of yellow liquid in its neck was all that remained. As I lifted the mug to my chapped lips, booze splashed into my eye. A flake of the asbestos paper from the crumbling stall's roof dropped into my drink.

"You going to drink that, gringo?" Emelio asked as he lit another joint.

The nasty fluid flowed over my lips, stinging their small cracks. I caught the chunk of soggy roof in my teeth and spat it into the puddle. The hazy cone of my headlamp's light dropped from Emelio's face down onto the muddy water. The asbestos floated on the surface, slowly spinning. Through a hole in the roof, water once again tapped on my forehead with eerie, repetitive precision.

A week later, the teeth of my crampons scratched their way down the quartz and granite face of my consolation peak, Cerro Solo, as I carefully rappelled. I loosened my grip and allowed the thin cords to slide through the belay device as I carefully balanced on a narrow ledge. Two moves later, I stepped back onto the glacier, crunching into the firm névé.

The last section of unpaved road approaching El Chalten, Argentina. When complete, the new accessibility of the young village will likely change it forever. (Brian Irwin photo.)

As we descended, my mind slid back into a courtyard with flowers but was sharply ejected back into reality as my crampons snagged a small imperfection in the glacier. Up the valley, thick precipitation shrouded the towers. For just a moment, the weather's lasso loosened. Pink light quickly melted the spires' granite tips out of the storm, allowing the giant ice mushrooms on Cerro Torre's summit to glow brightly for a second before they were erased by the churning grey curtain of clouds.

Far below me, on the other side of the massif, rain was falling on the tattered roofs of the stalls. I was content. I had summited. I had slipped through a tight window of fine skies that few short-trip visitors to the massif are blessed with. I knew I was lucky and not just for the climb, considered by most to be easy by Patagonian standards, or the weather. As my hands flipped coils of new rope over my head, I visualized a trashed piece of cord floating in a puddle. I imagined the roar of the wind tearing through Fraile. I pictured that drafty cabin that Rodrigo's family calls home, literally swaying in the wind. And my ears rang with the sharp laughter of three boys in wet sneakers splashing in the mud.

CLIMBING KIDS

"**L**OST LEDGE. IT'S perfect. It's just down the road. That's where you should take him," Joe Cote told me when I asked him for a good place to take a two-year-old climbing. The charismatic, old-school first ascensionist of our local New Hampshire ultra classic rock climbs, like Cannon Mountain's *Moby Grape* (5.8, III), took a sip of beer. His captivating smile quivered. My son Andy dashed around the party wearing his four-inch-long new rock climbing shoes.

"Rock climbing . . . yeah!" he squealed as he darted between my legs, lassoing Joe's and my feet with a length of yellow climbing rope. Joe is a master of teaching kids to climb. He's not a guide or a renowned instructor. Rather, he's an inspiration, a mentor. Kids may learn how to climb from Joe, but more importantly, they learn climbing is fun.

From a toddler's viewpoint, Lost Ledge is no place to let your guard down. Easy by adult standards, it's over two hundred feet of the gnarliest forty-degree, bolted, low fifth-class slab climbing in the East. And it seems committing and alpine. A full twenty minutes from the road, for my young son, this monstrous approach hike calculates to an age-adjusted time of over ten hours. I was going to do it in a single push, and I was confident he was ready. An expedition like this would require me to pack at least the ten essentials: two sippy-cups of juice, three diapers, baby wipes, water, and a security blanket.

Andy had free soloed[†] the stairs over a year earlier and had all the moves wired. Having toproped a full pitch on nearby Whitehorse Ledge the week before, he was clearly hungry for a bigger challenge. The night

---

[†]   Free soloing a climb refers to climbing alone, without the use of bolts, protective climbing equipment or ropes. It is the most pure, risky form of climbing.

before the climb he hardly slept. He screamed to have his pants changed, for more milk, and a stuffed beluga whale I bought him in Talkeetna, Alaska. Granted, he never sleeps well, but that night was different. I could see in his face that he was thinking of the climb, imagining his assault of the harrowing granite face. He was like a horse waiting for the gates to open.

I got a late start. Breakfast in town first, followed by two snack breaks got me to the trailhead by 11:00 a.m. Lost Ledge is not a misnomer. After the expected twenty minutes of hiking, we found ourselves bushwhacking up a streambed. We were lost, and there wasn't a ledge in sight. An hour later I thrashed up a steep slope, monkeying from tree to tree in order to pull myself through the dense vegetation. Navigating by GPS, it was not until the screen read "twelve feet to waypoint" that I ejected from the thicket, with Andy on my back, and first saw rock.

Andy's face was striped with brush burn from bristly branches. He was in a good mood; somehow, he'd napped most of the hike in. Sitting on a boulder, he eyed the obvious aesthetic line above us. As his little mouth worked a bite of Cliff Bar, I could see him thinking, reciting the climbing techniques in *How to Rock Climb* I'd read him as a bedtime story a few days earlier: "Tension off that flake, stem the corner and pull up into that pocket. Rest, then mantle into that dish." He was anxious to conquer the route.

Andy and the author in Yosemite, California. (Jay Mathers photo.)

After assembling a complicated belay system, Andy and I cast off. We climbed the first forty feet and pulled into a basketball-sized pothole. Andy dropped his butt into the hole and took a rest.

"Oooh, that was hard, Daddy," he declared.

We shook out and headed up the last stretch, a committing wall of improbable 5.1 knobby granite horns. Andy was getting pumped. I reminded him of the classic alpine tale every climber recites in his or her head when on the verge of failure or collapse—*The Little Engine That Could*. A few quiet grunts squeaked out from under his tiny helmet as he made the last few moves to the chains.

We start to climb because it's fun, but over time we keep climbing because it offers something more—something intangible, a connection with mortality and risk that makes us feel alive. It offers introspection, honesty, and challenge. It's not always fun. There's nothing fun about suffering in a snow cave at the base of a wall, awaiting stability of the snowpack above or dying winds in a hope to launch an ascent of what could be the best climb of your life, or your last. But suffering is sometimes a requisite part of climbing.

We cope with the suffering by talking to ourselves. We tell ourselves things like "It'll all be worthwhile" or "You've wanted this for your entire life and now you're here." These phrases scream in our minds as we limp up runout faces, settle for questionable bivouacs, or plod up the last few-hundred feet to the true summit. These hollering voices keep us alive as we drip sweat onto the tattered cables of old cams or pins as we drive the cold steel into granite. And sometimes, tragically, these words resonate in some climber's ears as they slip into the last sleep of their lives.

Climbing is a wonderfully simple and primitive act. It's one of the first things kids do after they learn how to walk. Climbing kids aren't born with the ability to understand the work or the suffering that may, for them someday, become part of their passion, that years later they'll spend a lot of money to climb a mountain that leaves them empty-handed and frostbitten and come back reporting it was the best trip of their lives. They don't understand that with a bad bushwhack, they just experienced their first epic. They haven't learned how to talk themselves down. But they have already learned the most important lesson of climbing: joy.

That night I lay in bed when Andy shouted out. I went into his room and found him sitting bolt upright.

"Daddy," he said as he flipped his security blanket over his shoulder, "I want to go rock climbing again."

I laid him down and tucked him in.

"You liked it?" I replied.

"Yea. Rock climbing is fun. Really fun."

Andy Irwin works his route in Yosemite, California, rehearsing the moves with intense focus. (Jay Mathers photo.)

KOZ, HE'S THE MAN

"ARE YOU SURE? I think it might be too much tent. And stove. And food."

Kozlanski looked at me judgingly. The twins from South Carolina chuckled and shook their heads.

"This is what we used in the Denali Prep course, and this is what we're taking up there."

The twins looked at me, flanking Kozlanski like supportive pillars.

"You 'The Man' Koz!" they exclaimed in unison. "Whatever you say goes!"

I was hard up for climbing partners. I was only in Jackson, Wyoming, for a few days; and things other than climbing the Grand Teton were on my agenda. When I trolled up and down the cooking shelter's tables, I thought I hit gold. Now I realized this might not be true.

I burst into the cabin, defeated, with a rejected tent in one hand and portable climbing stove in the other. My dog Marcy barked, then ran to my side. She gyrated and smeared against my thigh in a primitive attempt to win my love. She is a dumb dog. And poorly behaved. She sprinted out the door, violating the quiet experience I'd promised James, the ranch's caretaker. I packed my things and, with a nervous sense of doubt about the companionship I was about to enjoy, crawled into the creaky bunk, its plywood bowing under my weight.

I heaved as I passed the moraine. I was fit but feeling terrible. I didn't know these guys. I didn't want to bitch. I hadn't looked at the group gear cache as we divided it up. I trusted Koz to be fair. After all, he was "the man." At the lower saddle, I dropped my pack, my neck aching from its frameless design. I dumped its contents onto the ground. My clothes, a harness, two ropes. Koz dumped his as well. Two more ropes. The twins each tossed a rope into the kitty. Thomas, their friend, looked at me and rolled his eyes.

"Six ropes? Are more people coming?"

The twins looked at each other, then to Koz. He snickered and retorted.

"*Always* bring an extra rope. Especially on a trip like this."

That night I was lying comfortably in our enormous three-man tent, next to Koz. A candle lantern burned overhead, its weak light shining off the oily coating on three empty beef jerky wrappers next to Koz's head.

"Do you have a topo of the route?" I asked him.

He handed me a thick, heavy hardback copy of Leigh Ortenburger's *A Climber's Guide to the Teton Range.*

"It's on page 93, I think."

I didn't know how to respond. We'd xeroxed copies of the route map the day before, but Koz had also elected to bring the whole hardback guidebook that encompassed the entire range. I rolled over, folding my wrist under my neck as a pillow as I read, wondering what else Koz had in his pack in addition to his extra rack, spare stove and three times the necessary food. An object flew across the tent and struck my leg. A sharp pain erupted in my tired calf.

"What the fuck was that?"

"The good book, my friend. The only book."

I glanced down at my sleeping bag. The dull yellow light passing through the tent walls illuminated the cover of the New Testament between my legs.

"No thanks, Koz, I'm not religious. I don't read the Bible."

His eyes darted toward me. The twin fortunate enough to share the tent with Koz sat up in astonishment.

"Tonight you do." They both slowly lay back down.

We left camp at around four in the morning. Thomas and I decided to climb as a party of two; Koz would lead the twins. The previous night's rain, followed by a cold snap and high winds had glazed the upper Exum Ridge, our planned line of ascent, in a sheet of ice. Koz coached the twins, reassuring them that "a bit of ice would make it easier."

Thomas and I glanced at each other, knowing that in such conditions, the friction climbing on the ridge would be a certain hazard, if not a catastrophe. Instead, we elected to traverse around the ridge to a steep couloir that led to an alternative route, one that we thought would be easier to climb in icy conditions. We were taunted by Koz as we left their group.

"Good luck, suckers. You're going to get lost!" he gloated, the twins cackling in tow.

Hours later, Thomas and I found ourselves on the summit block. Koz and the twins had not made it onto the ridge proper. We could see them far below us, wandering around the loose rocky slopes that are avoided by most parties. They were heading back to camp where we'd meet them after our descent.

Climbing the *Idaho Express Couloir*, Grand Teton, Wyoming. (Brian Irwin photo.)

Thomas and I walked out together. My knees were sore even though my load had been lightened by tents and gear left with Koz and the twins as they planned their next assault. They were staying another night. They reported the variation they took wasn't off route. It was "recon." Tomorrow was summit day for them, according to Koz.

As Thomas and I slapped our tired feet against the trail, I listened to my MiniDisc player, its familiar sounds scratching their way out of cheap earphones.

"How did you meet up with those guys?" I asked. "You're pretty normal. Why do you hang out with Koz anyway?"

Thomas stopped and looked over his pack's lid toward me.

"He's 'the man,' isn't he?"

FLOATING THE SWAN

M Y RESIDENCY WAS criticized by some of our alumni for coddling its doctors in training. I didn't agree. I was learning how to become a rural family physician in Maine's Great North Woods. Upon graduation I'd be cast out into the world to save lives and deliver babies with no one but my hospital administration and the opportunistic eyes of malpractice legal firms to criticize my work. If I messed up in residency, there was someone around to catch it; if I messed up after residency, a mistake would only be caught after harm was done. Or someone was dead. So as I trained, I didn't mind a little hand-holding.

Dr. Mike Lacomb didn't hold hands. One of the most astute teachers at the Maine-Dartmouth Family Practice Residency, he was charming and Socratic. He was gentle in his approach as he taught us in the intensive care unit, his realm of expertise, where he was not only an intensivist but a cardiologist. He dropped complicated questions and cases onto the laps of residents, expecting either the right answer, careful research, or both. He was a kind man who delivered our keynote graduation speech, a review of a millennium-long genealogic tree that linked each of us to the first physician in recorded history. There wasn't a dry eye in the house.

I respected Lacomb so much that I was reluctant to call him for help with patients unless I had no choice. Unless a patient's health was at stake, I had the courage to call Dr. Lacomb only with medical problems that I thought were complex enough to make even him take pause. If I could look it up and fix the medical issue myself, I would. I wanted him to think I was smart.

One afternoon I sat in the ICU, comfortable in loose teal scrubs but weathering the sensation of swollen, heavy eyelids from the lack of sleep that was generated by the continuous care I'd provided an elderly woman the entire night prior. She had congestive heart failure, a condition whereby the heart's ability to pump is overwhelmed by the amount or pressure of the blood it must mobilize. The result was shortness of breath and fluid accumulation in her lungs. I'd carefully balanced her medications overnight and been able to aid her body in excreting the extra fluid. She'd stabilized, and I felt proud that Dr. Lacomb had been able to sleep, uninterrupted.

My patient also had emphysema from smoking. And pneumonia. And a history of lung cancer that led to an operation five years earlier in which one-half of her right lung was removed. Her shortness of breath was the result of many factors, and the management of these issues was complicated. If she filled with fluid from her heart failure, I'd need to give her medicine to make her urinate off the excess. If her blood pressure dropped from those medications, she'd need more IV fluids. Unless her blood pressure dropped from her pneumonia having spread infection to her bloodstream, then she'd need different antibiotics and medications that constrict her blood vessels. Unless they were already constricted, then she may need steroids as it might actually be her emphysema that was the primary problem. And the complications went on and on as they do with many critical patients.

Shortly before I was to turn over my shift to the next resident, the patient became very short of breath. She was adamant about her desire to avoid a mechanical ventilator, and her tearful family begged me to comply with her undocumented wishes. I collected all the lab results and X-rays I needed, reviewed them, and with a gulp, paged Dr. Lacomb.

I told Dr. Lacomb I needed his help. Primarily I wanted to make sure he'd reviewed the data and been ensured that I, the kid, was making the right decisions and doing everything I could to save the life of a woman who, regardless of who her doctor was, would likely not survive. I suggested we feed a Swan-Ganz catheter into one of her heart's main arteries, allowing us to directly measure the pressure in that vessel. It wouldn't save her life, but it would provide the information needed so that we, Dr. Lacomb and I, could try.

I'd just placed a Swan-Ganz catheter for the second time in my life the month prior. There's an adage in medical training: "See one. Do one. Teach one." Most medical procedures can be comfortably learned after two successful attempts. And thanks to Lacomb's guidance, I'd been successful on my last Swan.

To place the catheter, one must first position the patient and then sterilize the upper chest. An enormous needle is driven into the vein, which is the diameter of a magic marker and runs just under the clavicle. Into that needle a wire is threaded. The needle is withdrawn, and the wire is left hanging out of the patient's bloody chest. Using that wire as guidance, an intricate catheter is "floated" into the vein, through the heart's chambers, and into an artery where it will measure pressure. Aim too high on that initial needlestick and the patient will wail in pain. Aim too low and their lung will collapse.

Lacomb watched silently with an outstretched lip, a sign that he was concentrating intensely, as I drenched the patient's chest in iodine, prepping her for the procedure. The family waited in the waiting room. I draped the clavicle, felt the landmarks, and turned to Lacomb. He put on one sterile glove, glided his finger across the aseptic, slick skin, and nodded at me. With his other hand, he peeled off that glove, inverting it with a loud snap as he ripped it off his hand. He turned to me and with a thin smile said, "Page me when you're done." He walked out.

The patient was barely coherent and hadn't moved the whole time. The nurse assisting us, who I'd known for years, turned to me with wide surprised eyes. In my training program, we were referred to by our first names until we'd graduated; there was an unspoken culture that although we were already doctors, we hadn't yet proved it. "Ready, Brian?" she asked as she handed me the syringe. I grasped it with my gloved hand, the interior powder wetting out quickly from perspiration. A bead of sweat rolled from my armpit quickly down my clammy side. Carefully I floated the Swan, collecting a series of measurements and drawing my conclusions. I called Dr. Lacomb and reported the facts, finishing with my hypothesis.

The patient's lungs were full of fluid at this point, and her breathing had deteriorated. We'd been operating on the theory that heart failure was her primary problem and that she'd need to diurese (the term for being medically induced to urinate off extra, retained fluid). Surprisingly, her first set of measurements revealed low rather than high, overloaded pressures in her heart's arteries. We'd been wrong. She didn't have too much fluid in her system. She didn't have enough. And the fluid on her lungs wasn't fluid. It was pus from her pneumonia.

Dr. Lacomb told me to "write some orders," which I did. I ordered aggressive IV fluids from the nurse, more powerful antibiotics from the hospital pharmacy, and three coffees from the cafeteria. As I watched the patient's rising and falling chest, her shortness of breath improving quickly, Dr. Lacomb came into the ICU and quickly reviewed the orders and the data. He turned to leave, stopping three paces away. He turned toward me, and with a nod he said, "Nice job. Thank you, Doctor."

The nurse approached me minutes later. "I know you have your coffee, but is there anything else I can get you? Dr. Irwin?"

Part Two

Rime and Rocks

Cirrus cloud over Rima Rima, Cordilla Blanca, Peru. (Brian Irwin photo.)

Freeski or Die: New Hampshire's Mount Washington

"JUSTIN . . . CHRIS ON ground channel."

"Go ahead, Chris."

"Patient's packaged and ready to lower."

"Lower."

"Lowering," Chris replied.

His hands steadily loosened as they fed ice-encrusted rope through two fat carabiners attached to a complex snow anchor. The rescue litter scratched its way across an icy slope, slowly dropping three hundred feet to the next anchor, where the painstaking task of lowering a battered, fallen skier down "The Fan" in Mount Washington's Huntington Ravine continued.

Three hours later, I sat in the back of the U.S. Forest Service's 1998 LMC snowcat with the fallen skier as we noisily bounced our way down to Pinkham notch where an ambulance awaited. The spinning tracks kicked up snow onto our laps as I relentlessly forced the patient to answer and reiterate simple questions, like his address and his dog's name, in an attempt to evaluate his mental status and ensure it was not deteriorating. Chris Joosen was driving. He is the head USFS Snow Ranger on New Hampshire's Mount Washington. Sitting in the passenger seat was Cutler, who is not only Chris's best friend but also the avalanche dog for Mount Washington Avalanche Center.

After a turbulent ride down the mountain, the crimson snowcat rounded the final bend in the trail, carefully crossed one last bridge and pulled into the parking lot. The patient remained coherent the entire ride, arguably more so than his exhausted rescuers. He was loaded into the ambulance and taken to the local hospital, where he was treated, released, and went on to fully recover. Joosen pulled the snowcat into its garage and headed home. A day like that is tiring, but not uncommon for him and his crew. Before the winter is over, they'll execute a dozen rescues like this one. And every patient fared well in the end.

Chris Joosen, lead ranger, and Cutler. (Brian Irwin photo.)

Joosen is the most recent in a lineage of U.S. Forest Service rangers who provide avalanche advisories and rescue in the famous Tuckerman Ravine, neighboring Huntington Ravine and, if needed, in the Gulf of Slides. Chris is responsible for five thousand acres of avalanche terrain and for overseeing three other snow rangers and a volunteer backcountry ski patrol. Quite a bit of responsibility, but in Chris's five years, he's proven to be a worthy successor to Brad Ray and Leavitt Bowie, the latter of whom was the first snow ranger back in 1952.

The Mount Washington Avalanche Center is the only avalanche forecasting program in the Eastern United States. Affectionately known by locals as "the rock pile," Mount Washington is a stunning sight with its broad shoulders, steep, tempting couloirs and giant snowfields that draw skiers from all over the country. The great terrain makes this area appropriately popular; however, the mountain has notoriously awful weather. This combination presents unique challenges for Joosen and his crew compared to western avalanche centers.

Avalanche runout, *Hillman's Highway*, Mount Washington, New Hampshire. (Photo courtesy of Brian Johnston and the U.S. Forest Service.)

"Our ravines are relatively small areas but are used for recreation by a large number of people. Mount Washington's high winds[‡] and heavy snow loading are daily occurrences," Joosen says. "Upslope flow can turn two inches of snow into a two foot slab in little time. This, plus our high concentration of visitors, means that if any instability exists, someone is likely to find it."

This alpine playground is only a short approach from the car and is less than three hours from Boston, but in terms of objective hazards it is just as serious as any other big mountain. Tuckerman's slopes are leeward, allowing them to catch over a hundred feet of wind-transported snow a year, the perfect setup for natural avalanche activity. The upside is that Tuckerman and even the Gulf of Slides (depending on the year) can be reliably skied into the month of June. Frequently at least one "skiable" iceberg lasts in the ravine until July or August. Although it may only be large enough for one or two turns, each year people trudge up the trail with boards on their backs in an attempt to be the last skier of the year to schuss the ravine.

Active avalanche control, such as the utilization of explosives to micromanage different aspects of the ravine in an attempt bring down unstable slopes, is no longer part of Joosen's program. There was a time when the rangers' emphasis was different. During the 1950s, the snow rangers would actually close Tuckerman Ravine during and after storms, times when Tuckerman was most likely to avalanche. Conversely the Gulf of Slides and Huntington Ravine were largely unmonitored. That changed in 1964 when two climbers, Hugo Stadmueller and John Griffin, died in an avalanche in Huntington Ravine. Starting that year, the USFS avalanche advisory was expanded to include Huntington. The Gulf of Slides, however, was left unpatrolled and unforecasted, which is how it remains today.

[‡] Mount Washington holds the record for the highest ground wind speed ever recorded on earth—231 mph on April 12, 1934.

Early avalanche control. (Photo courtesy of the New England Ski Museum.)

Closing Tuckerman may have been a useful way of preventing avalanche casualties, but it did nothing to propagate potential slides. In 1958, the USFS began active avalanche control, initially by using rifles and machine guns to shatter the icefalls that ring the ravine, hoping that the icefall would release unstable slopes. In 1966, the USFS bought one of the first Avalaunchers ever produced. The eight-foot cannon was used to launch avalanche-triggering shells onto unstable slopes, but its use in the ravine was discontinued in less than a year, partially because of an accident in which a shell prematurely exploded in the barrel and injured two rangers. Active avalanche control in the ravines was abandoned, being replaced by the current policy of visitor education and daily avalanche advisories.

While many things have changed on Mount Washington's eastern slopes over the decades, many things have not. The Hermit Lake caretaker's cabin sits on the site of the now-incinerated "Ho-Jo's" warming hut, so named because of its similarity to the building style used by the Howard Johnson motel chain. Across the courtyard adjacent to Hermit Lake is the backcountry outpost for the USFS ranger headquarters, which has gone essentially unchanged for the last fifty years. Snow rangers still post their avalanche advisories on old-fashioned brown wooden slatboards. And they still oversee Mount Washington's ski patrol.

Avalanche slats, Hermit Lake, Mount Washington, New Hampshire. (Brian Irwin photo.)

The Mount Washington Volunteer Ski Patrol (MWVSP) was founded in 1947 by Swampy Paris and Bill Putnam in response to the growing number of skiers in Tuckerman and the surrounding ravines and the need to organize the USFS's manpower for more efficient rescues. Today the patrol is still the only backcountry ski patrol in the Eastern United States and the only Eastern U.S. patrol that consistently works in avalanche terrain. Like Swampy, who didn't stop patrolling until the 1980s, most patrollers are veterans of the job. The average patroller has been volunteering for over a decade. One member of the MWVSP has been ski patrolling for sixty years.

The patrol stays busy. On a given spring day, thousands of people may pack the ravine, carrying with them varying stores of experience, equipment, and common sense. During a particular day in 2006 there were ten injuries, many serious, in a single hour. In the last twelve years, five people have required rescue after falling into "the hole," a deep (sometimes one hundred feet) crevasse that forms in the center of the bowl each year as a result of undermined snowpack from meltwater. In 1994 a twenty-two-year-old woman died after skiing into a crevasse. Incidents like these require patrollers to not only be proficient in first aid, but also in ski mountaineering and alpine climbing skills.

Kevin LaRue, one of the most tenured members of the Mount Washington Volunteer Ski Patrol. (Brian Irwin photo.)

The increase in accidents on Mount Washington over the last twenty years is in part due to the current ease of access. In the early 1920s, when Tuckerman first became popular, it was accessible only by a long trip up a twelve-mile stretch of steep, unplowed road to Pinkham Notch Camp (where today's Tuckerman Ravine Trail starts), followed by a three-mile thrash up the Cutler River. By the end of the decade, Route 16 to Pinkham Notch was maintained in winter, making the approach much more bearable. In 1932 a fire road was built to Hermit Lake. Two years later the Civilian Conservation Corps built the classic John Sherburne Ski Trail. The Gulf of Slides Ski Trail and a fire road into Huntington were cut a short time later.

By the mid 1930s, so-called ski trains were running regular shuttles between Boston and New Hampshire, bringing thousands of skiers into Mount Washington every spring. Tuckerman, and to a degree the neighboring ravines, had become booming celebrations of skiing, the country's newest aristocratic sport. It had been twenty years since Mount Washington was first popularized by Fred Harris, the founder of the highly active Dartmouth Outing Club (DOC), and the ravines were rapidly becoming more developed.

The first GS race in the United States. This famous photo was erroneously identified during the printing process as a Dartmouth-Harvard race, when in fact it is the Franklin Edson Memorial Race. The photo title has never been corrected, even on prints sold today. (Photo courtesy of the New England Ski Museum.)

First descents of the more prominent couloirs fell to pioneers such as Dick Durrance and Warren Chivers during the early and mid-1930s. Durrance, Chivers, and many other members of the DOC used Tuckerman Ravine as a training ground for their university's ski team. Skiers from Harvard did the same; and within a short time, Tuckerman's unique walls were used for a multitude of downhill and giant slalom races (Tuckerman is touted to be the birthplace of GS), including university competitions, Olympic trials, and the famous Inferno Races.

The first Inferno was run in 1933. It was an exhausting descent from the summit to Pinkham Notch and was won by Hollis Phillips in just over fourteen minutes. A second Inferno was held a year later with Dick Durrance shaving two minutes off the record. The third Inferno in 1939 was the race that put Mount Washington on the international ski map.

Hannes Schneider was a prolific Austrian who emigrated to North Conway, New Hampshire, bringing with him a revolutionary new technique of ski instruction. He is often referred to as "the father of American skiing." Toni Matt worked as one of Schneider's ski instructors and was the winner of the third Inferno, shattering the previous best time at 6:29 from the summit to Pinkham. Herbert Schneider is Hannes's son and was in Tuckerman on the day of the third Inferno. He told me his recollection of the famous run.

Dodge's Drop, the steepest line in Tuckerman. (Brian Johnston photo.)

"I was just a kid and wasn't skiing in the race. So Toni asked me to hold his lunch. He told me, 'I'm going to ski right over the lip[§], all the way to the bottom and turn only three times.' He skied off the summit cone, soared over the lip, landed, and in a blink, he was gone. Later, at Pinkham, he was asked, 'What happened to your three turns?' Toni said, 'I used them all up at the top!' Then he gave me half his sandwich."

Any plums left to be picked on Mount Washington were snatched by Brooks Dodge II, who spent a decade pioneering a dozen scary descents, many of which are more popular today as technical climbing routes than ski lines. Now, fifty years later, his son, Brooks Dodge III, still lives in the area and can often be seen gracefully repeating his father's tracks down *Dodge's Drop* or the *Dutchess*.

It's hard to make new history on a mountain where history was made. Today, there aren't any first descents left to be had on Mount Washington. Instead, skiers enjoy what does exist: many fifty- to sixty-degree couloirs, potential for over four thousand feet of vertical from summit to pavement, and a unique social scene. Lunch Rocks, the giant pile of boulders on the edge of Tuckerman, is the party headquarters on a sunny day. When the sun goes down, the bash continues at Hermit Lake. Music oozes from the shelters; people stumble around with a bottle in one hand and a burrito in the other, looking for the privy. Some Tuckerman veterans go all out. Crews of fraternity brothers with matching T-shirts (Trashed at Tuckerman, '04), sets of fine china set out on a tableclothed picnic table complete with champagne and even kegs of beer manage to wander up to the Ravine on a nice weekend.

The Snow Ranger's cabin is a virtual museum with its tarnished brass weather instruments and yellowing photos of Brad Ray patrolling Tuckerman Ravine. Pasta sauce bubbles on the old stovetop, occasionally building to an audible pop that flings red flecks onto the mint green tiles that line the cabin's kitchen. Like everything else on Mount Washington, the patrol and the ranger's weekly pasta night is a tradition. The rangers talk about last week's accident in Huntington while some of the patrollers practice tying knots or read magazines. I chew garlic bread quietly as

---

[§]   The lip is the steep rollover just right of the center headwall icefall. Most years it
        is around fifty degrees and drops seven hundred vertical feet to the bowl's floor
        in under a quarter of a mile.

Tuckerman, Brad's German shepherd, who was Cutler's predecessor, plops his tired head onto my lap. Brad retired from thirty-five years as head snow ranger, only to turn around and join the ski patrol.

The boot-ladder to Tuckerman's Lip on a busy day. (Photo courtesy of Brian Johnston and the U.S. Forest Service.)

After dinner, I retire to the patrol cabin. As I lay in my bunk, a propane lantern throws dim light across the room onto the coarse pages of my book. Raspy snoring from the top bunk is overridden by the brutal gusts of wind bludgeoning the pine paneling that separates my head from the harsh winter night. I turn off the lantern and crawl into my musky sleeping bag. As the lamp's fragile ash mantle fades, I screw my earplugs in and listen as the slow crunching of expanding foam drowns out the wind. I'm enveloped in silence while the wind continues to load snow onto yesterday's sun crust. I think to myself, *Tomorrow's going to be a busy day.*

Hermit Lake's Snow Ranger cabin and the now-retired LMC snowmachine. (Brian Irwin photo.)

THE CRADLE OF
AMERICAN ALPINISM

The east side of Mount Washington, New Hampshire. *Damnation Gully* (NEI3, III) is the long, rightmost couloir visible in the distance. (Photo courtesy of Brian Johnston and the U.S. Forest service.)

PAUL CORMIER LOOKS like a mad scientist. Incredibly fit at fifty-six, his graying hairs squirt out of the sides of his brown fleece hat, their tips frosted with rime and frozen sweat. The normally sarcastic and funny Cormier is stone-faced as he fights constant eighty-mile-per-hour winds on the east face of New Hampshire's Mount Washington. Airborne cord whips around him; pack straps snap at his hood as he struggles to build an anchor at the top of *Damnation Gully* (NEI3, III). His young partner, Tim Martel, leans into the wind as he prepares to be lowered into the spindrifting shaft. The pair hardly speak. Not because of the wind. Because they're looking for a couple that are probably dead.

The previous day, Damian McDonald and Susanna Santala left the Harvard Mountaineering Club's backcountry cabin on the east slope of Washington. Santala had never climbed before but had rented equipment and was fit. The party left late in the day to climb the one-thousand-foot *Damnation*. Making slow progress, they topped out at dusk but faced increasing winds and poor visibility. Seventy-mile-per-hour gusts and below-zero temps made descent impossible. The party was crawling against the wind using axes for forward progression. Exhausted, the pair sought shelter behind a few small rocks.

Rick Wilcox approaching the *Black Dike* (NEI5, M3, IV) prior to its second ascent. (Photo courtesy of Rick Wilcox collection.)

While Cormier and Martel labored, other search parties scour the mountain, one by the trade route *Lion's Head*, another across the Alpine

Garden, a flat area above Huntington Ravine. Accompanied by a few members of the Androscoggin Valley Search and Rescue team, Cormier and Martel are part of North Conway, New Hampshire's Mountain Rescue Service or MRS. Founded in part by legendary climber Rick Wilcox, his group of volunteers has operated as the primary technical rescue team in the Mount Washington Valley since 1972. As the long-time president of MRS, Wilcox's efforts these days usually revolve around dispatching and coordinating rescue efforts rather than ticking the first or second ascents of stunning test pieces like Cathedral Ledge's *Repentance* (NEI5, III) or Cannon Cliff's *Black Dike* (NEI5, M3, IV) like he did in his youth.

Mount Washington is best known for its awful weather and its unique alpine atmosphere in an otherwise hardwood-choked Northeast. In addition to its possession of the world's highest land wind-speed record, the mountain has an average daily wind speed of thirty-two miles per hour. In winter, two-thirds of the days typically yield hurricane-force gusts. Typically, 650 cm of snow or more falls on the peak per year; this snowfall coupled with temperatures that have reached negative forty-five degrees Celsius make a dangerous brew for climbers, both in terms of exposure and avalanche potential. Despite the fact that in July nearby Cathedral Ledge can be sweltering, the highest temperature ever recorded on Washington is twenty-three degrees Celsius.

Perhaps Mount Washington's weather is why this mountain, a mere 6,288 feet high, has seen so many climbing accidents. However, for the same reasons, it's one of the country's best training grounds for alpine climbing in the higher ranges, drawing out a patchwork of talented climbers from the North Country to New Hampshire's White Mountains. Local youngbloods like Freddie Wilkinson (who lives in a shed) and Kevin Mahoney share belays with mentors like Steve "Father Time" Larson (FA *South Face* Mount Foraker, Alaska) and Tom Hargis (FA *Northwest Ridge* Gasherbrum IV, Pakistan). During rescues, nationally known rescue instructors like Alain Comeau spit complicated anchors into the ice like darts while humble hard men like Kurt Winkler tenuously tend to loaded litters as they scratch their way down icy slopes and crumbling rock bands.

Many of the accidents on Washington are a result of the hill's unique weather, poor human judgment, or both. Overall, the snowpack on the eastern side of the mountain tends to be more unstable. Avalanches are common, and although more of an issue for skiers, they often play a role in climbing accidents.

In November of 2002, eleven antsy climbers, ascending in three separate groups, were climbing in Tuckerman Ravine. The topmost party, consisting of three soloists, topped out as a second party climbed the moderate ice below. A third party was at the base of the "open book," Tuck's fattest early season pitch. An avalanche released above all three parties and swept the line, leaving the roped party of two hanging from a screw anchor midroute. Five climbers escaped the slide, but four others were buried in avalanche debris in the bowl of the ravine.

Dave Lottman climbing early season ice on Tuckerman Ravine's Headwall, Mount Washington, New Hampshire. (Rob Vandergrift photo.)

Two of the buried climbers were recovered quickly. Two more were not as fortunate. Even with fast response time from the snow rangers, the avalanche dog and local hut caretakers couldn't save the lives of the two deceased, one of whom was found by following the climbing rope he was holding (but not yet tied into); the other was found by the rescuers avalanche probe line. The slide had run over one thousand feet.

Avalanches also strike Huntington Ravine, where most of the technical climbing is. In 2008, a party, again climbing underneath another party, was swept by a slide while climbing *North Gully* (NEI 3, III). The lead climber was knocked off and sent fifty feet down the gully. His unanchored belayer was yanked up and into the gully, hauled in a pulleylike fashion by the upward force of the rope that ran from him up to a piece of protection and back down to the falling climber. Thankfully, that fixed protection the leader had already clipped held, leaving the two hanging from either end of the rope, battered but alive.

Jeff Lane after topping out on *North Gully* (NEI3, III) in Huntington Ravine. (Photo courtesy of Brian Johnston and the U.S. Forest Service.)

Alpine exposure is a major reason why Washington stands as the hub of eastern mountaineers today. It is also this facet that drew early climbers to its impressive slopes. The eastern side of Mount Washington boasts two huge glacial cirques, the famed "backcountry" ski block-party, Tuckerman Ravine, and neighboring Huntington Ravine. Huntington's face is the steepest on the mountain and is split by two primary buttresses, Central and Pinnacle. The forbidding dark Pinnacle Buttress was more than a stepping stone in climbing history; it was the first roped climb accomplished in the White Mountains and quickly became a litmus test for the era's alpine frontiersmen.

Pinnacle Buttress was first climbed in 1910 by a party of four led by George A. Flagg. While technically ascended in roped fashion, the party used a simple clothesline, not a climbing rope, to protect the steeper sections and solo climbed the remainder. The entire climb was carefully documented in Flagg's sketchbooks, which confirmed not only the topography, but also the cruxes, which were rated as "bad" or "very bad."

Eighteen years later on October 14, 1928, Robert Underhill, Ken Henderson, and three others made the first complete ascent of the *Northeast Ridge of the Pinnacle* (5.7, III), which went on to become a modern-day classic and one of the East's premier alpine rock routes. More difficult variations were later established

An unknown climber leading the third pitch of Pinnacle Buttress' *Northeast Ridge* (5.7, III). (Brian Irwin photo.)

by Underhill and Fritz Wiessner. Described in a 1928 issue of *Appalachia*, this seven-pitch route's crux is a dirty chimney that party member William Allis climbed "after much struggle and a certain amount of buoyant language." Other difficult steps were overcome by having one climber stand on the shoulders of another. Regardless of this technique, the popular climbing clothing of the generation was a derby hat, jacket and tie, demonstrating the era's interpretation of what it meant to climb in good style.

Other quality alpine rock routes and scrambles dot the apron of Mount Washington; however, they are largely either undocumented or underdocumented. Unnamed dihedrals and cracks ranging from 5.6 to 5.10 line cliff bands teeter above Tuckerman Ravine and just under the Lion's Head buttress, the spine of which makes up Washington's winter mountaineering trade route. Three buttresses—which go by local nicknames ranging from The Three Cathedrals to Larry, Curly, and Moe—crown the Boot Spur Ridge, hovering over some of Tuckerman's steepest couloirs, which themselves are fine snow climbs. These oft-neglected gems harbor surprisingly solid rock, and their lack of beta provide climbers with a sense of adventure and exploration.

One of Washington's most remote, exposed cirques is the giant, 1,800-foot-deep Great Gulf. A stout 6.5 mile approach makes climbing the ravine's one-thousand-foot headwall a serious endeavor, despite the moderate nature of its ice routes, which are poorly documented and no harder than NEI III. Regardless, the first recorded ascent was impressive, requiring twice the distance of the modern approach as the road that makes the cirque more accessible today had not yet been built. It was in 1905 that the giant north face was conquered by Appalachian Mountain Club employees George Whipple, Warren Hart, and Herschel Parker. Parker is perhaps best known for defrauding Frederick Cook and Robert Peary's false claims to the first ascent of Mount McKinley. The climb required laborious step chopping, a fall during which, according to Whipple, would have resulted in "the rest of [their] lives sliding down a snow slope."

Better known and more frequently visited than the Great Gulf, Huntington Ravine is home to some of the country's most important early ice climbing accomplishments. The opening of the ravine's ice climbs truly did usher in a new period of advancement in American alpinism. Dartmouth climbers John Holden and Nathaniel Goodrich tackled *Central Gully* (NEI 2, II) in 1927. Within two years, neighboring *Odell's Gully* (NEI 2-3, II) was climbed by its namesake, Noel Odell, a visiting British geologist. Cutting steps, he and his party surmounted steep ice bulges and sustained alpine ice, conquering what was, at the time, the boldest climb on Washington. Huntington's five other mixed snow and ice climbs fell over the next two decades. *Damnation Gully* was the last to be climbed, in early 1943. While it is the longest alpine route in Huntington, even today it is often overlooked by climbers in pursuit of one of New England's most classic, aesthetic lines, *Pinnacle Gully* (NEI 3+, III).

The first ascent of *Pinnacle Gully*, formerly known as "Fall of the Maiden's Tears" is, according to northeast climbing historians Guy and Laura Waterman, "the landmark climb of prewar northeastern ice." Various Yale and Harvard climbers, including Bradford Washburn, eyed or attempted the climb; but it wasn't until the relatively inexperienced Julian Whittlesey and Sam Scoville kicked steps up to the top of *Pinnacle* that alpinism took a leap forward, as the Watermans state, in terms of "vision and mental attitude."

Early ascent of *Odell's Gully* (NEI3+, III). (Rick Wilcox photo.)

For the next four decades, *Pinnacle Gully* would stand as the most feared and difficult winter route in the Northeast. However, like most ice routes that had been established during the era, *Pinnacle's* reputation for challenge fell hard after Yvonne Chouinard introduced America to short tools, innovative picks, and the revolutionary front-point technique, all of which made climbing steep ice considerably easier. Using this arsenal, *Pinnacle Gully* was climbed for the first time without the need for step cutting by Jim MacCarthy and a large party, which he led, during the winter of 1970.

Chouinard demonstrating his step-cutting technique. (Rick Wilcox photo.)

By today's standards, most of the climbs, both rock and alpine, on Mount Washington are considered moderate. Huntington's bulky Central Buttress does hold a few more difficult, stellar lines, like *Mechanic's Route* (5.10b, III) and *Roof of the World* (5.11d, III). These two routes were opened by Ed Webster, the first solo and the second with Kurt Winkler in 1987. While most of Mount Washington is climbed out, there is still some new route development. Although like Webster found on *Mechanic's Route*, ancient pins (whose discovery led to the route's name) and even manila slings are occasionally discovered, lending doubt to anyone who tries to lay claim to virgin ground. The most recent documented new activity are a trio of steep lines, including an aid crack, that climbs the huge lichen-splattered, overhanging wall of Pinnacle Buttress which were established in 2004.

Despite the moderate difficulty of the climbs on Washington, they frequently turn into horror shows with the addition of cataclysmic weather, blowing fog, and avalanches. In January of 2008, a climber was killed by an avalanche on *Odell's Gully*. In 2001, a ruptured ice dam sent the former Harvard Mountaineering Club hut's caretaker, Ned Greene, down *Damnation* to his death. In 1982, Albert Dow, a member of the Mountain Rescue Service, was buried by an avalanche while on a search-and-rescue mission to locate two missing climbers. They survived. Dow did not. A rescue cache in his honor now stands in the floor of Huntington Ravine.

As rime slowly grew on the rocks around McDonald and Santala, their body temperatures continued to fall. It was seventeen degrees below zero without windchill, and SAR teams were in a race against time. Both climbers were hypothermic; and McDonald, in single boots, had suffered severe frostbite, partially in an attempt to shield his partner from the incessant winds. Surviving an open bivy on Mount Washington is unlikely, as is a break in the weather. Miraculously, in the early morning hours, both of those improbabilities occurred. The clouds thinned, allowing Marc Chauvin, an Everest veteran and local guide, to spot the pair, bludgeoned by the wind but alive. A thousand feet below, barely visible, the red cross on the door of the Dow cache peeked through the trees for an instant before the lifeless gray fog of Mount Washington once again swallowed it.

SLIDING ON THE CROWN JEWEL

R OB TICE IS a friendly thin man with a shaggy beard and a sharp jawline. He sits by the window, sipping hot coffee from a pale green coffee mug with a chip in its rim. As the steam rolls across his face, he squints into binoculars as he stares up at the enormous headwall that's flanked by fifty-degree gullies and capped by the twenty-inch-wide "knife edge" ridge.

"Looks nasty out there. You can't even see the *Cilley-Barber*," Rob says, alluding to New England's classic alpine ice climb.

Ben Mirkin approaching Katahdin. The giant North Basin lies right of center. (Brian Irwin photo.)

Rob is the alpine ranger on Maine's Mount Katahdin. He spends each wind-whipped winter in a drafty cabin seated vulnerably in the mountain's giant South Basin. It's not a common ski destination; in fact it's not a common *winter* destination. Katahdin is a long way from anything. While not as remote as Quebec's Chic Chocs, it still takes two days of skinning to get from the trailhead at the southern gate of Baxter State Park (which encompasses Katahdin) to the South Basin of Katahdin, and another day to make it to the rarely visited North Basin. But once you're there, it's well worth the effort.

Ski mountaineering on Katahdin is truly an exercise in self-reliance and expeditionary skills. It's always been that way. First skied in 1926 by Arthur Comey, the peak has a number of routes on all sides of the mountain; however, the history of its first descents are nearly impossible to compile. Katahdin has been quietly, humbly, and covertly skied by a die-hard local crew of skiers over the years that focused on fun, not fame. Even though some of the more obvious lines remained unskied until as late as the 1980s, first descent credit is still often unknown.

The Chimney, Katahdin's longest couloir. (Brian Irwin photo.)

Most of the steeper, aesthetic couloirs reside on the east side of the mountain in one of two huge glacial cirques. Even the shortest approach route requires a fifteen mile ski and 2,400 vertical feet of climbing just to get to the base of the gullies. Depending on the line chosen, you may then have to climb for hours up steep slopes, alpine ice, and third-class rock to reach the point where you can click into your bindings for any number of one-thousand-foot runs that range from fun to frightening.

Access to Katahdin is not easy. Baxter is tightly regulated; among eastern skiers, Baxter's winter rules are notorious and are widely despised. The rigorous registration process, which includes such hoops as a four-member team minimum size, mandatory checkpoints, and even a gear review with the ranger, does feel more like trying to get a tube of toothpaste through airport security than a ski mountaineering safety or overuse prevention policy.

Despite the difficult access and regulatory process, there have still been forty-six recreation-related deaths in Baxter since 1962. Even Mount Washington, focus of the book *Not Without Peril: 150 years of Misadventure on the Presidential Range,* has had fewer accidents during that period. However, as Tice pointed out during my interview with him a few years ago, "[Baxter] has very few *winter* incidents."

"We average two deaths per year in the park, but most of those are during summer and most aren't even on the mountain," Tice said.

"So far in the winter of 06/07 there have been no deaths. In fact, there has been only one mentionable winter incident *at all* in 06/07, and that was a dislocated shoulder that was self-evacuated by the patient's skiing partners."

Jamie Pollette skiing afternoon corn, Great Basin, Mount Katahdin, Maine. (Brian Irwin photo.)

"[Mount Katahdin] draws a hard-core user group. You'd be hard pressed to find anything this remote in the White Mountains," Tice said, referring to the mountain chain to the west that includes Mount Washington. "The winter policy is rooted in the 'safety in numbers' motto. With four skiers, your group can be self-sufficient, which can be the difference between surviving and dying."

Because of Katahdin's remoteness, the Baxter State Park Authority defends its rigid winter visitor policy that, according to Jensen Bissell, current park director, "is important for the safety of both visitors and would-be rescuers." While the winter registration process may work reasonably well despite its unpopularity, not all of Baxter's policies make this much sense. Perhaps the most perplexing land management policy is Baxter's annual closure of the park from April until June as well as for two months in early fall. Bissell commented, "Trails tend to be wet and vulnerable in the spring and fall. Closing them during this period allows them time to regenerate. To get to the skiing in spring, one would have to hike over a mixture of mud, ice, and rock. Another problem is that [in fall] some visitors come prepared for summer conditions but the weather reverts to winter weather in a matter of hours, which can be unsafe."

Katahdin's summit. (Brian Irwin photo.)

Weather on Katahdin can change quickly. Having been smacked down on the Knife Edge, I can attest to its fickle potential. Weather on the mountain is worst in winter when the park is open to skiing.

Paradoxically, Katahdin is off limits in the spring when the snowpack is more stable and unlikely to avalanche. The mountain is closed just when it's becoming safer for skiing and even climbing. This fact, which Bissell does not deny, seems to contradict the park's policy of protecting visitors from dangerous mountain conditions.

Baxter State Park has a carry-in, carryout policy, a ban on music, alcohol, or any backcountry use at all during the shoulder seasons. While these rules do protect the land, many people feel the park's execution of founder Governor Percival Baxter's goal to keep the park wild and preserved is somewhat imperfect. This is perhaps most exemplified by the park's lack of gray water disposal sites or structures, even in Baxter's most heavily used backcountry campsites such as Chimney Pond.

Despite the ban on late spring skiing or Baxter's quirky policies, Katahdin remains one of the most worthwhile destinations in the country. A trip into Baxter is truly a delight. There are no crowds and no noise. You feel alone, because you are. The experience is uniquely alpine and removed from the rest of the world. It's a feeling you can't get anywhere else in the East.

Ben Mirkin descending The Saddle, Mount Katahdin, Maine. (Brian Irwin photo.)

Aside from the wastewater issue, Baxter is pristine. Granted, there aren't extensive powder bowls; but this amazing massif offers up an eye-popping selection of huge 1,000-1,500 ft. couloirs that spill into easier fifteen- to twenty-degree snowfields. From the summit, slots like the two-thousand-foot *Chimney* make you shake your head, wondering if you're in Maine or on Canada's Baffin Island.

The difficulty of the routes on Katahdin varies dramatically from twenty-degree cruisers down the Abol trail or in the Great Basin to the extreme technical descent routes of the remote North Basin or the *Chimney Couloir*. Many of the steeper lines require rappels over ice bulges or exquisite caution to jump-turn in fifteen-foot-wide slots that run out into jumbled glacial moraine.

Last winter, Ben Mirkin and I stood next to each other at the top of an unnamed gully on Katahdin's South Basin. We'd been there for five minutes, standing in silence, as we stared down the plunging stripe of snow.

"Steep, isn't it?" Ben said to me.

"Really steep. You first or me?" I replied.

"Mmmm . . . You." Ben paused with temptation. "Wait . . . me. I'll go first."

His tips flexed in the wind as they hung over the edge of the cornice. Ben leaned back slightly and then pitched forward, springing into the narrow chasm. His skis darted perpendicular to the fall line, his knee dropped, bouncing off the crusty, rotten snow; and the gully echoed the loud scrape of steel on ice. Two more turns and he was over a bulge, out of sight. I stood alone, with my skis pointed into emptiness. I could hear my heartbeat in my ears. I took a deep breath, leaned forward, and jumped.

Mirkin skiing the Great Basin, Mount Katahdin, Maine. (Brian Irwin photo.)

The Beast of the East

LINCOLN MCNULTY'S RESCUE was the first time I'd laid hands, and even eyes, on Mount Katahdin. Being "from away," I was a flatlander, new to New England. I remember the pathologically giddy sound of his voice when he first greeted me as I pulled my wary body onto his ledge that night: "I got summer teeth. Some are here, some are there."

He laughed, the dried blood on his face cracking on his cheeks as he smiled. The cone of light from my headlamp cut through my breath's vapor and cast shadows across his face. Clear liquid sparkled on his face. It appeared to be leaking from his nose and bludgeoned ear, raising the possibility that it was cerebrospinal fluid. Six of us from two separate rescue teams teetered high on the face, leaning into the wind for balance. We'd been paged out six hours earlier, at 9:00 p.m., after hikers had reported the distant screams of Lincoln's girlfriend as she cried for help after their accident.

Rain pegged the top of my helmet, slowly becoming more fine and persistent as I worked on Lincoln's injuries. Gusts of wind blew dust into my eyes and face. Most of the rescuers had driven for hours to get here and were exhausted. As we worked in a tangled mess of rope and loose rock, the rhythmic sound of helicopter blades grew louder as the Black Hawk glided into the cirque.

The chopper floated up, then down a few times in an attempt to find us as we sat patiently in the gray light on cold, wet slabs. It drifted slowly closer to the huge alpine face, feathering its pitch to ease the blades into the shallow depression between the Armadillo and Flatiron buttresses. Gusts of wind pushed the helicopter toward the wall. Raindrops fell from above, met the Black Hawk's rotor wash, and accelerated like pellets onto our bare hands. McNulty lay immobilized in the litter, wind whistling through his missing front teeth, inflating his cheeks. His Mylar blanket exploded into shreds under the power of the wind.

A National Guard medic lowered, swinging with the wind until he touched down next to us. One clip of the fat cable and he and Lincoln zipped off the ledge. As the helicopter slid out of the valley, the rain stopped and the sun rose, throwing hazy pink light over the dense green forest of northern Maine and onto the granite ridge above us.

The Armadillo Buttress, Mount Katahdin, Maine. (Brian Irwin photo.)

The second time I climbed on Katahdin was more relaxing. A pleasant romp up the *Diamonds* (5.6, II) followed by some scrambling to the top of Maine's highest peak. At 5,267 feet, Katahdin is the pride of Baxter State Park and the northern terminus of the 2,175-mile-long Appalachian Trail. It's also the most alpine climbing arena east of the Rockies. The sharp fin of rock punches four thousand feet skyward from Maine's flat conifer carpet, its sides falling away into glacially eroded basins. The granite is mostly solid and holds a number of natural lines with good protection, thanks to New England's harsh winter freeze-thaw cycles. While word of mouth has popularized a few stellar moderates like the *Armadillo* (5.7, IV), a substantial amount of the technical terrain on this mountain is either unclimbed, undocumented, or both. Only here can a one-thousand-foot face like the Taber Wall hide from development, its clean, steep, well-protected routes going years between ascents.

"Scottish" conditions, Mount Katahdin, Maine. (Brian Irwin photo.)

While Baxter's aforementioned restrictions are notorious and detested by most climbers, they shouldn't be despised without understanding their cultural background. Northern Maine is remote, rich with culture, wildlife, and wilderness. It's untamed land, and Percival Baxter, former Maine governor who established Baxter in 1931, loved it for that reason. The park administrators who strive for preservation in hopes that the land will "be used to the fullest extent, but in the right, unspoiled way" have grown up fishing, hunting, and hiking. Not climbing.

Another reason Katahdin has remained under climbing's radar is its North Woods ethics and strict political regulation. It's an old-school area. No bolts. No pins. No tat, a term climbers use to describe unsightly weathered nests of old nylon webbing and cord left behind by previous climbing parties as they've retreated from routes. Katahdin has no dedicated guidebook. The only consistent source of beta is a collection of handwritten descriptions by the first ascensionists, its thin yellowing pages carefully filed in a decaying binder in the desk of the Chimney Pond alpine ranger. His drafty backcountry cabin sits in the giant South Basin,

Katahdin's most frequented climbing area. The East's longest ridge climb, the two-thousand-foot *Pamola IV* (5.5 variations up to 5.8, III), darts from the pond to meet the Knife Edge, the wild narrow arête that makes up the skyline. Dripping down from this sharp spine are the two-thousand-foot *Waterfall Buttress* (5.5, IV); *The Flatiron* (5.9, III); and in winter, dozens of long ice climbs. The *Cilley-Barber* route (WI 4+, IV) was one of the boldest ascents in the country when first climbed in 1973. Even today, this route is committing, taking two days of skiing even to reach its base.

The author climbing Mount Katahdin's *Pamola IV* (5.5, III). (Conrad Yager photo.)

While the classic climbs are prominent, a plethora of other, more obscure rock lines of all difficulty levels stripe the cirque. But you won't find any beta on them. For example, almost all of the dozen or so routes (many at least 5.10) that ascend the *Cathedrals,* a set of free-standing pillars on the north side of the cirque, remain documented only in the minds or journals of active local first ascensionists like Ben Townsend, who is a former Chimney Pond alpine ranger, and Bob Baribeau.

Baribeau is elusive, a tall, thin man with a quiet voice and a bushy beard. One of the East's strongest and most unassuming climbers, he's witty and confident. Baribeau could easily write a guidebook to the peak or share information about his routes on the Internet, but he won't. When asked how many first ascents he's climbed on the mountain, he said, "There are a lot of people who would answer that question, but I'm not one of them." Baribeau is one of many who have been climbing here for years—quietly, humbly, and for all his own reasons. "Katahdin is a wilderness area where climbing is adventure," he says when I asked him why there's no published guide to the peak. "Keeping it that way is part of what keeps the place so special."

Some from his generation want to preserve the spirit of adventure at Katahdin. Others keep quiet because they don't want their land abused or overused. Most of them are simply modest climbers with nothing to prove. Baribeau is one of many who live by the Katahdin code of ethics: keep your mouth shut.

Katahdin's South Basin is huge but is swallowed in scale by the neighboring North Basin. Likely the most alpine setting in the East, this enormous cirque seems transplanted from the Canadian Rockies. Giant crumbling ridges encase alpine tarns; lichen clings to the rocks. Gnarled dwarf pines poke from the deep caves between balanced boulders. To the east, a carpet of green stretches to the horizon, devoid of roads, interrupted only by the occasional flash of sun reflecting off a distant pond. A four-and-a-half-mile hike and one-hour bushwhack from the trailhead, the basin's impressive Taber Wall is flanked by scores of slabs, ridges, and gullies. While the beta binder at Chimney Pond holds accounts of five routes on this monolith, Baribeau confirms there are many more. "There are over twenty routes, with half of them more difficult than 5.10," he says. "As far as the names and the location of them, I'm not ready to share any of that."

There actually may not be much to share. While the North Basin sports scores of routes and the South Basin holds even more, the actual first-ascent histories of many have been either lost in time or poorly documented via five-sentence descriptions in 1940s and '50s issues of *Appalachia*, the country's longest-running mountain journal.

"It's remarkable," says former ranger Townsend. "You're six pitches up what you think is a new line and you come across an old iron pin or ring in the most unlikely place." A few years ago, Townsend found an anchor of sun-bleached antiquated manila slings. Baribeau once discovered a circa 1940 wooden wedge jammed in a crux crack.

Not everyone keeps Katahdin secrets. Peter Lataille, an old-fashioned climber who's been one of the mountain's most active developers, records his routes in the Chimney Pond book. Lataille is an amusing man who chuckles as he recounts his old climbs while shaping surfboards in the shed out back of his home in Hampden, Maine. A publication-worthy topo of his and Townsend's 2005 route *Magdalana* (5.9+, IV) is the binder's most recent addition. This eight-pitch line climbs straight up the Taber Wall to join his other recent contributions like *Los Nuevos Videntes* (5.11+, IV) and *Little Bear* (5.10+, IV). But even Lataille isn't sure if these are actually new routes. "On Katahdin, the best way to tell if it's a new route or not is the rock quality. If there's no loose rock, chances are Baribeau has already done it."

The impressive Taber Wall, North Basin, Mount Katahdin, Maine. (Brian Irwin photo.)

The Northwest Basin is a thousand-foot-deep cirque that holds multiple steep buttresses and was first climbed by Arnold Wexler and partners, probably in the 1940s, although no formal documentation of the ascents exist. Wexler was an early climber who was very active on Katahdin through that era. Also a brilliant engineer at the National Institute of Standards and Technology in Gaithersburg, Maryland, Wexler is considered to be the creator of the dynamic belay, which he tested extensively at the National Bureau of Standards and Technology. Wexler climbed all over the world, ticking achievements that range from the second ascent of Mount Sir Sanford (which came thirty-two years after its first ascent), British Columbia, to putting up over fifty routes from West Virginia's Seneca Rocks to the Kashmir.

As a Maryland native, I had met Wexler when I was a boy. I wasn't a climber then, rather a nerd who presented a jelly bean and coat hanger model of DNA at the National Bureau for my science club. Wexler was one of the judges. I'm sorry now that I didn't take the opportunity to interview him after I'd become interested in climbing. As with many of his other accomplishments, details of Wexler's Katahdin climbs lay buried in history books or in the grave. He died in 1997. According to Rick Wilcox, Wexler was one of the only climbers to thoroughly explore the Northwest Basin. While others may have taken stealth trips into the remote area, Wilcox says, "There's been virtually no real climbing activity in that basin in decades."

Young Peter Cole, one of Rick Wilcox' regular climbing partners during the years he developed many New Hampshire classic climbs. (Photo courtesy of Rick Wilcox collection.)

Wilcox is somewhat of a Northeast climbing historian. He's a fit short man with a graying moustache who otherwise looks almost the same as he did thirty years ago. Every day, this fifty-six-year-old walking history book can be found dispensing advice as he works the sales floor of International Mountain Equipment, North Conway, New Hampshire's climbing retail epicenter and local hangout, which he's owned and operated for over twenty years. Wilcox coauthored New England's only comprehensive ice-climbing guide, *Selected Climbs in the Northeast*, and has compiled more route information and historical data about Katahdin's ice climbing history than anyone. He's pasted together route descriptions of almost fifty ice climbs in the South Basin and nine more in the North Basin. A small handful of these he lists as mixed climbs as they follow summer rock routes, like the improbable *Hanta Yo*, which weaves through the intimidating grade IV Taber Wall at 5.7. For this reason, Wilcox's ice guide is the closest thing Katahdin has to a rock climbing guidebook.

Wilcox is perhaps best known for his climbs of eight-thousand-meter peaks like Makalu, Cho Oyu, and Everest as well as first ascents of many New Hampshire test-piece ice climbs. He was also involved with the first technical rescue on Katahdin back in the winter of 1972. Wilcox recalls, "We got the call in North Conway at noon. In a matter of hours, we were in a Cessna, and by that night, we were at Chimney Pond. Early the next morning, we climbed up and located the frozen body of Tom Keddy. His partner, Paul Dibello [who later lost his legs to severe frostbite from the epic], stayed with him while team leader Bob Proudman and the other members of their party went for help. Conditions were awful: minus twenty temperatures with hundred-mile-per-hour winds that didn't die down for a week." The accident occurred on a route now referred to as *Pamola's Fury* (WI 3+, III). It later got its second ascent, and first complete ascent, by Wilcox and John Bouchard.

Percival Baxter entrusted the land that comprises Baxter State Park and Mount Katahdin with a very strict set of bylaws. He had a specific vision for this land, and the current land use policy remains in place to protect this. Initially, the park was set aside only for the use of Maine residents, a policy that was later discarded. Regardless, the park authority still holds Baxter's mission of the park sacred. Open recreation, especially the kind that can be dangerous, doesn't fit into the current or past administration's interpretation of the park's purpose. In Baxter, climbing is still considered a "fringe" activity, one that can only cause trouble, just like it did in 1972.

However, the park's attitude toward climbing seems to be evolving. Thirty years ago, a party could only access Katahdin in winter if the members presented a certified letter from a bonded rescue team that vowed to bail them out if need be, as well as letters of medical clearance from each climber's physician. While that regulation has changed, change takes time, and time can seem to stand still in Northern Maine.

"This isn't a climber's park," says Rob Tice, current Chimney Pond alpine ranger. "It's managed the way it was meant to be, the way Percival wanted it to be." A climber himself, Tice would know. He spends each wind-whipped winter in the frigid basin, enforcing the rules that he knows make climbing Katahdin more than a physical challenge.

Tice has been proactive in loosening Baxter's stranglehold on the East's most protected alpine climbing area. He has successfully lobbied against ridiculous policies like the recently overturned regulation that winter climbers had to climb in parties of no fewer than four at any time on any given route. For years, such misguided rules have forced larger climbing parties to stay banded together, instead of allowing them to follow the practice of dividing up to climb independent parallel lines or variations. This technique is the norm for most alpine climbers and helps avoid subjecting lower parties on narrow routes, like the *Cilley-Barber* (WI 4+, IV), to icefall hazard.

Percival Baxter stressed proper land management and preservation. Arguably though, his vision has been misunderstood. The park spends an enormous number of man-hours enforcing their winter registration process, yet this exhausting winter permit system lacks a mandatory lecture on minimal impact land use or any visitor education regarding leave-no-trace ethics, which seems odd considering the park is closed for four months out of the year to allow the land to recover. Even on Denali, which does not require a gear check or minimum party of four members, climbers are issued registered garbage bags and fined if they are not returned full.

This isn't to say Katahdin looks like a litter box. It's very well preserved, making for an amazing alpine experience. That is, if you can get in. On most summer days, the Chimney Pond lot is full and its gate closed by 7:00 a.m. There are strict cutoff times for embarking on a hike or climb. Summer camping in the Northwest Basin is limited to one night, which, given the one-way eight-hour approach, greatly stifles climbing. In winter, camping is prohibited in the Northwest Basin altogether. The North Basin itself is also off limits to camping year round, making a trip into the cirque a huge day.

While these policies may have helped protect the land, they are resented by many climbers. Brad White, director of the International Mountain Climbing School in North Conway, New Hampshire, describes Baxter's policies as "disappointing." "It seems as if [the Baxter State Park Authority] is deliberately trying to discourage climbing on the mountain, especially in winter," he says. "These rules aren't necessary. Such overregulation keeps some of the most high-end climbers from enjoying that amazing mountain."

Among the most detested policies are the camping regulations, including a ban on planned bivies.

"Bandit camping has been going on for years up here," the lanky Townsend, now a lawyer in Augusta, Maine, says as he recalls his time as alpine ranger. "Many of the bold routes couldn't have been done without a bivy, at least not by the parties that climbed them." That said, the park's limits on camping don't make ascents there impossible—it just makes them burly. Townsend has proven this by climbing some of the most committing lines on the mountain without rogue camping.

Bending Katahdin's rules has led to important route development. In 1982, Peter Cole and Marc Chauvin established a stunning ice climb that followed a plumb line from Chimney Pond directly to the summit. While they didn't directly disobey the orders of the ranger, they left at 10:00 a.m. in marginal conditions, an act that would be grounds for ejection from the park if they were caught. They swiftly climbed the *Chauvin-Cole Route* (WI3+, M2, III) and were back by dark. This route is now considered a classic.

Every day, the Chimney Pond Ranger evaluates the weather forecast. The day is posted as class one through four in summer or green, yellow, or red in winter. Higher numbers or warmer colors indicate high winds, precipitation, or other factors that lead to dangerous conditions and potentially restricted use. Sleet, for example, is justification for a red rating, which may mean the mountain is closed to all use. While possibly helpful for hikers, this system has serious flaws. In winter, the ranger at Chimney Pond is rarely a climber with any training in snowpack stability. I once saw a calm bluebird day after a long storm that left thirty inches of slabby snow on the steep, avalanche-prone couloirs posted as a green day, which means "favorable conditions."

The current restrictions on Katahdin are frustrating to accept as a climber. Current equipment and training allow safe mountain travel that wouldn't have been possible decades ago. Even the essentially unregulated ravines of Mount Washington, which see literally hundreds of times more visitors than Katahdin, are just as clean and preserved; and they see dramatically fewer accidents per visitor. So are the regulations helping?

Katahdin is, and hopefully will always be, a place where self-reliance is first priority. This isn't an area where people learn to climb or even a place to go cragging. Katahdin is big, and its climbs are committing. While some of the best alpinists have cut their teeth on Katahdin, others, like McNulty, have lost theirs. This is adventure climbing. On Katahdin, if you want beta, climb up and get it.

EASTERN TREAT

BEFORE I MOVED to New England, I made an annual pilgrimage from the Mid-Atlantic to ski Tuckerman Ravine. As fun as it was, it was always a little disappointing to drive twelve hours, ski for three miles, hike for an hour, and crest the bowl to find seven hundred people with radios, Bar-B-Qs, and no fresh powder in sight. On a typical spring day, the snowcat-packed trail to "The Bowl" is so crowded that it has more potholes than postholes. Earlier in winter, when the crowds are thinner and the best powder is falling, so are avalanches on Tuckerman's steep slopes. Less than an hour from Tucks is a little-known backcountry gem without any of those inconveniences, full of great runs, glades, and quintessential New England skiing—less the crowds.

In search of northeastern powder stashes without a carnival atmosphere, some friends and I explored the Phillips Brook Backcountry Recreation Area during a January full moon. Sadly, Phillips Brook is now in the process of being reclaimed from the land-lease company that manages the area by the logging company that owns the land. Despite its association with the paper industry, the Phillips Brook Area was an exceptionally preserved chunk of real estate, remote and beautiful—especially in the winter when the logging activity is at a minimum. The area is over twenty-four thousand acres and includes seventy-five miles of trails and, at one time, eleven yurts. Many of the wider trails are logging roads, mostly inactive. Cut deep into the mountains, these trails used to provide some of the best access to glades and chutes for backcountry skiers, snowshoers, and snowboarders in the East.

Driving through the gate, I followed the snowy access road along a cascading trout-filled stream for many miles. The only traffic we encountered during our thirty-minute approach consisted of a few dogsled teams. Not only was there no evidence of crowds, there was also little obvious evidence of widespread logging. The woods near the road were thick and what harvesting had been done was performed in a selective manner, leaving some trees standing. The Phillips Brook was weeded for valuable trees, not clear cut, preserving the wilderness sensation. We were very surprised to find such wild country so close to the crowded outlet-lined streets of North Conway.

From the trailhead, we skinned up moderate terrain to the Millsfield Yurt, which sat in the middle of a perfect glade. Below the yurt dripped a series of narrow, steeper chutes, which hung on the slopes much like the classic old-fashioned ski trails that wind with, not against, the fall line at old-school Vermont ski areas like Mad River Glen. Scattered birch groves dotted the hillsides, interspersed with hardwoods and pines, the perfect eastern blend. There were even a few cliffs to be jumped, buried in the forest.

The Eastern backcountry is known for its junglelike density, but around Millsfield the trees were perfectly spaced, reminiscent of the famous American Airlines commercial showing Billy Kidd bouncing through the trees as he skied the "champagne powder" pillows at Colorado's Steamboat Springs. After a day of cutting up two feet of fresh powder in this area, we settled into the yurt, sharing Jim Beam and Top Ramen with two wool-clad, bearded canoe builders from Maine. We sat on the deck sipping bourbon at 2:00 a.m., watching the amazing green and pink ribbons of the *aurora borealis* ripple in the sky.

The next morning, while skiing the glades, we met a group from Vermont who was passing through during a traverse. Ben, the group's leader, was skiing on old wooden telemark skis and well-broken-in leather boots. His soles were smooth, like a seasoned pair of combat boots. He propped his bamboo poles into his armpits, brushed the snow off the bottom of his wool slacks (which he wore with neon pink gaiters), and asked us, "Been to the backside yet?"

"Nope . . . wait, what backside?" I ignorantly responded.

"Over the top. C'mon."

We followed Ben and his two brothers behind the yurt, up a narrow gully, through the thick brush, and finally to the ridgeline. It was easy to see why the yurt was built at a lower point on the hillside; there was no view from this ridge. We continued to bushwhack for about a mile. Finally, the ridge opened up. To the east, plenty of fine lines jumped out at us as the thick trees melted out into perfectly spaced glades, far from the reach of the closest logging road. Not too steep, we cut lines in and out, gaining speed through the glades, stomping through the thicket, and letting loose again as the density decreased. We finally climbed back up to the ridge and traversed to the yurt where we then skied out to the parking spot. The trip out was almost as fun as the glades. Except for our ascent tracks, the twenty-foot-wide trail was blanketed in fresh, untouched powder. After two miles of fresh turns, we were back at the truck.

We settled into that night's yurt, the East Branch Yurt, one of the few yurts to which you can drive. We laid out a route for the next day to the Dummer Ridge Yurt, eight miles south. From there we would head west to the Long Mountain Yurt, finishing a traverse of the range that makes up the spine of the Phillips Brook. We had bottles of wine, steaks, potatoes, and ice cream saved in the truck for the last day of the trip; but after seeing the amenities of the yurts, like Millsfield, we were kicking ourselves for leaving the good stuff at the car the previous evening and settling for dried noodles. The yurts had all the silverware, pots, and propane needed to whip up a huge feast without bringing anything but the food itself.

That night the sky was clear enough to see the starry band of the Milky Way. It was cold, but a ripping fire kept the yurt toasty. As we were dozing off, we heard the soft, deliberate crunching of snow on the other side of the canvas wall that separated our bunks from the frigid night air. I got up and cracked the door. Under a full moon stood two moose, a bull and a cow. The bull sported a gigantic rack that easily scraped the ten-foot mark. He was no more than four feet from the door of the yurt, staring directly into our eyes. Under the bright moon, his huge nostrils spewed steam into the cold night. I shifted my weight in my seat to reach for a camera. The floor creaked and the moose ran. We went back to bed. In the morning we found the entire area trampled with hoofprints.

The Long Mountain Yurt, Phillips Brook Backcountry Recreation Area, New Hampshire. (Brian Irwin photo.)

After breakfast, we skied up to the Long Mountain Yurt. Situated at 3,615 ft., Long Mountain was the highest yurt in the area. This area had much more to offer than the previous zone, and the setting was spectacular. A four-mile ski up the Jodrey Brook Trail from the valley brought us to the face of Long Mountain. Two long traverses through wide glades and we were on the ridge, looking back on the valley below. After passing a steep chute that descends to "the Granite Shoulder," the trail wound through the trees and emerged on the far side of the ridge. The yurt sat in a clearing that gaped at the north face of Mount Washington, Mount Madison, Mount Adams, and the lesser peaks of the White Mountains.

Ben said this was the best skiing in the Phillips Brook drainage. He claimed the mountain's higher elevation held more powder, a scarce commodity in the middle of the notorious eastern midwinter thaw. It was true. The snow was well over five feet deep. After dropping our packs at the yurt, we backtracked up to an unmarked path atop the ridge named the String of Pearls Trail. We skinned for about a mile across the undulating ridge. The tree canopy was thick, and I was growing skeptical that this was the open, "classic Phillips Brook skiing" of which we were told. Fearing I was going to have to settle for a tour of the ridge, I was pleased to see the thick forest on the downslope aspect of the trail thin out and give way to an entire mountainside of perfect glades. I went one way, my friends another, and we didn't see each other for an hour. Eventually we passed each other at a brook crossing, took a few more runs, and returned to the yurt. The sun set just behind Long Mountain, and a brilliant pink lit up the heavy clouds that had slid into the valley to the south, leaving the snowy peaks of the Presidential Range spiking through the mist like islands in the ocean.

After our feast, we headed back to the String of Pearls Trail. The moon's glow sparkled off the feathery, fragile crystals of frozen dew on the ground, a phenomenon known as surface hoar. The moonlight was so bright we never turned on our headlamps. After two runs, we sat down on a log to have a sip of coffee. I gripped the thermos with both hands and took a sip. Steam rolled across my face. Down the hill, very faintly, we heard the crisp crunching of snow.

Part Three

Running Deep

Rainbow Trout, Madison, New Hampshire. (Robert Irwin photo.)

A Quality Day

THE MOUTH OF Washington State's Barnes Creek was a productive place to fish in the early season. Idyllic and sapphire, its clear water spilled out of the temperate rainforest, winding through mossy mounds of earth and giant Paleozoic-sized ferns on its way to Lake Crescent. Hungry, energetic trout clustered at the river's entrance to the lake, loitering just below the submerged gravel bar where the cold water sank to the depths of the lake bed. Blind strikes on nymph patterns were common and thrilling enough, but when the sun set each night and the evening hatch erupted, the smooth water surface transformed into a popping layer of activity. Bats would drop out of the trees and clip the lake, plucking infant insects from the air just above its surface. The trout would rise to the surface with certain, sometimes acrobatic, fervor to attack the night's hatch. And some nights, my fly.

By July, the jet skis churning up the water's surface, in combination with the summer sun, sent any worthwhile fish running deep into colder, quieter water. The productivity of my favorite fishing spot had dried up, so I sought out a new river. Not being a local, I relied on the advice of those who were, and I would come to find out that almost no one in the area was interested in much beyond timber harvesting, let alone fly-fishing. Defeated, I drove an hour into town to find some advice.

Port Angeles had only two fly shops, which wouldn't have been bad if the sum of the two added up to half of my local shop back in

Maryland. It made me homesick. I've always felt a certain connectedness to the water I've fished back east. I know those creeks well. I've casted into the same riffles of some of those streams a hundred times, perhaps more. I've caught fish out of a specific hole when I was nine years old and pulled another fish out of the same hole twenty years later. Here, many thousand miles west, I yearned for the feeling I had when I fished local waters. At home, it felt like the rivers were mine.

The first shop I visited was twenty by thirty feet. The white pegboard walls were streaked with rust stains from the naked ceiling's leaky pipes. There was, at most, one or two of each item, including fly patterns. The thin inventory was evenly spaced on rickety card tables in an attempt to give the illusion of a well-stocked store. The young man who worked there sat at a trying bench with his back to me. He was crouched over the vice, working on a masterpiece egg pattern.

"Excuse me," I said.

"What?" he replied, without turning around.

"I was wondering if you could give me pointers on good local water," I hopefully asked.

"I don't fish around here," he said. "It sucks."

So I found myself two blocks down the street at the "Quality Fly Shop." Quality was well stocked, perhaps too well. Inventory, at least when you are stocking the capes of dead animals, operates on the principle of diminishing returns. It is possible to become so "well stocked" that browsing halls of dried carcasses becomes intimidating and overwhelming. It felt like shopping in a slaughterhouse. Gear was jammed into glass cases, reels stacked high like a house of cards, and graphite rods stood tall and dense like a forest of bamboo. The walls were layered three and four deep with plumes, wings, and entire birds. This truly was a mausoleum of poultry.

Despite the impressive carnage, Mr. Quality provided little quality fishing advice. When I asked him where to go, he replied, "That's a pretty tough question to answer. There really isn't anywhere to go." Discouraged, I chose to explore the Elwha River, ten miles upstream from where it emptied into the Strait of Juan de Fuca. I assumed it held fish based on the fact that Quality sold a fly pattern called the Elwha Exterminator, and the fact that I'd been told by a local that the river was rich with steelhead and Dolly Varden. The Elwha is a wide flow, seventy feet across, and as blue as Caribbean water. It looked promising. There were fast riffles, boulders with swirling pockets, and deep-cut banks with bubbling eddies. The sun was low in the sky, and there were only a few clouds kissing the tips of the surrounding Olympic Mountains. A caddis hatch was just beginning.

I carefully waded upstream, casting as I cautiously avoided slick boulders with my felt-soled wading boots. The river was much more swift and powerful than it appeared. Careful to maintain my footing, I worked up and across the river. The beautiful sky was starting to darken. Within five minutes, it was snowing. In July. Snow pounding down, a caddis hatch rising up, and I was casting across. The visual barrage was enough to take away my balance. Nervous, I backed up and climbed onto a boulder. As I did, the snow turned to a frigid, piercing rain.

Still hopeful, I focused on a pocket of water on the far side of the river where a cloud of caddis hovered over a pod of feeding trout. Having trouble achieving a drag-free float, I stripped more line. The current was strong; and no matter how I cast, angled my line, or added loops to my cast, I couldn't get my exterminator to achieve more than a second of still, lifelike float before it skated out of the pool. I continued to strip line, which was now bobbing around the base of my boulder. Using an exceptionally unrefined double-haul, I managed to land my fly in the center of the pocket. It floated perfectly for two seconds and then forcefully disappeared underwater, leaving in its place the bubble that is characteristic of a trout's strike.

My rod was low in the water. Suddenly I felt tremendous pressure from my rod hand. Line began to peel from the reel, sending a high-pitched, ratchet-tearing sound into my ears. My heart rate doubled, and thoughts dashed through my head. "Why hadn't I brought a camera? Where should I get this monster mounted? Is it a huge salmon or a steelhead? Would I even be able to land this fish on 6X tippet?" It was then that I noticed my rod was unflexed.

I looked down and found my flotsam pile of slack gone. Line was being torn from the reel at an alarming speed, disappearing under the rock on which I was standing. Strangely, the line was not emerging from the boulder, rather vanishing underneath it. Using my now-soaked flannel shirt, I grasped the line and stopped the peeling. I was unable to retrieve the line with any speed. It was firmly jammed. After twenty minutes of inch-by-inch, hand-over-hand progress while lying prone, on top of the boulder, my arms had grown tired and numb in the frigid water. I was able to free my line, having been seemingly dragged to the depths of the earth by brisk white water. My fly was gone.

Deciding this was no way to end the day, I hopped off the rock and waded upstream to slower water. Fewer than a hundred feet upstream, I took a careless step onto a slimy rock and got what I deserved: a few gallons of glacial meltwater in my waders. Ironically, just as I righted myself, the cold rain stopped, the clouds broke apart, and sun shone on the valley, pitching a rainbow over the adjacent peaks.

Swearing to myself, I trudged back to the car, which was resting on top of a hill, witnessing this whole exhibition. Before leaving, I drove a bit farther upstream to a campground overlooking the river. There I saw a man on the bank by a calm, deep pool. I approached him.

"Any fish in there?" I asked.

"Yep. I ain't caught none though."

"Caddis?" I inquired.

"Yup. That's the fly for here. My cousin caught a nine-pound Dolly yesterday," he bragged.

"Put him back?" I asked.

"Yup. Say, fella . . . why you all wet?"

"Long story. You ever heard of the Elwha Exterminator?" I probed. The man chuckled and shook his head.

"Good luck, son. You may need it."

I dripped my way back to my dust-covered hatchback and moved downstream, pulling over along the river at a picnic table overlooking a deep blue bend in the river. I laid my sopping layers on the hood of my car and sat down. The caddis hatch continued, and the trout were hungry here as well. Glancing up, I noticed a tattered paper sign tacked to a tree. It was on Washington State Wildlife Commission letterhead and it cited, in fine print, all the salmon fishing regulations for the river. Below it, a thin cardboard strip was nailed to the tree. It was weather-beaten and hard to read. Written in pencil, but legible only by the impression the lead left, it read, "This is your river."

A Bowl Full of
Cherries

I T WAS A boring bar, no more than fifteen feet long. Its smooth
oak shone from its lack of fine mug-tapping, bottle-clanking bar
conversation. At the far end sat a National cash register, the old brass
type with stiff petal keys and a crank on the right hand side. We used
it simply to hold the money; its ability to calculate had broken years
before and had never been repaired. The bar had no draft beer and no
jukebox. It never would. Britt, the lodge's manager, said those things
brought trouble.

This all suited me fine. I was a new bartender, trying to learn the
trade and memorize drink recipes. It also gave me time to learn my lines.
"Who won the game?" "I shoot a .357 too but prefer a .45." "Yep, you're
right. Things would run better in this country if we could just get rid of
the government."

Washington State's Olympic Peninsula was not widely developed.
The closest town to Lake Crescent Lodge, where I worked and lived, was
twenty miles away and had nothing but a few shops and a gas station.
The economy was weak. There were essentially no employment options
outside of the area's sawmills and timber harvesting. Some inhabitants
had never been off the peninsula. Most of the men who worked and
lived here were lumberjacks, as were their fathers, as were their father's
fathers.

What the peninsula lacked in financial riches it more than made up
for in culture. There was an age-old battle between the local "Indians"
and the white men over who had rights to harvest the already decimated

salmon run from the mouths of the peninsula's rivers. Positions of power rarely turned over, and they were never given to an Indian. The sheriff had been in office for twenty-three years. He was forty-two.

The history of the peninsula is well documented. All the shops in town had black-and-white photos behind the counters, some framed, some simply pinned to the walls. Most of them showed lumberjacks at work, or on break. Men with bushy beards leaning on their axes in front of enormous evergreens. Others sitting on felled pines nearly fifteen feet across. A pulverized tractor, crushed by a miscalculated cut, its operator scratching his head in wonder.

One day I was waiting to pay my bill at the nearby Hungry Bear Café. As my server sliced pie before ringing me up, I leaned in to peruse the old photos tacked to the walls. In the center was a particularly tattered image, clearly older than the rest, worn smooth, and smeared with fingerprints from having been passed around and shown off. It was of three men in wool hats and rough flannel coats, smiling. Two men were looking at the camera, the third off to the side with a corncob pipe in his mouth. Behind them stood two Indians pulling taut a stringer of five large trout. At the bottom edge of the coffee-stained border, there was cursive writing in pencil. It read, "The Boys."

It was a typical day at the bar. Five o'clock and I'd already read the paper twice. My first customer was an older man, perhaps in his seventies. He sported an orange NRA hat. He sat down, peeled off the cap, dropped it onto the bar, and ordered a screwdriver. Britt walked up.

"Hey, Joe, how goes it?" Britt inquired.

"Still livin'. You?"

"Other than my hip?" Britt replied, as he turned to me and shot me a look that begged for sympathy.

"Yea. How's that old thing anyway? You gotta just get that fixed," Joe lectured.

"I know. Go out smornin'?"

Joe took a sip of his drink, the first screwdriver I'd ever made. "Nah. Did yesterday though."

"Jack go?"

"Yea. But he didn't catch nuthin'." Joe turned to me, shaking his head. "Ol' Jack. He never catch nothin'."

"What did you catch?" I asked.

"Beardslee. Two of 'em. What a day," Joe bragged.

I had never heard of a Beardslee before and, honestly, was not sure at that point if it was even a type of fish. I inquired.

"Beardslee what, Joe?"

"Trout, boy! Where you been? The East?" Joe replied. Joe and Britt looked at each other and laughed. Britt often teased me, referring to me as a "flatlander" due to my Maryland roots.

"Very funny, guys. Where do they live? Here in Crescent?"

Britt chimed in, "Yea, but only down deep."

"Can you catch them on fly?" I asked hopefully.

"Nope," Joe replied," you gotta troll. You working tomorrow?"

"No," I answered, hoping that an invitation was coming. Joe could see the excitement on my face.

"We'll go tomorrow. Ten o' clock."

Joe was not just surprised that as a fisherman I'd not heard of a Beardslee, he was almost offended. He'd lived on the peninsula his entire life and seemed unaware that any other type of trout existed. Britt pulled up a stool. He and Joe enlightened me about the history of the serendipitous fish, how they live hundreds of feet deep, are very rare, and grow to be "as big as a man." Britt left for a minute, returning with a dust-covered scrapbook. He carefully flipped it open on the bar. We leaned in and listened to Joe's raspy voice as he narrated stories about each of the pictures.

Many photos were from the turn of the century, before Joe's time. He told us of the economic boom of the 1920s and how it affected the peninsula. Before any legitimate roads were cut to the south shore of Crescent Lake, where the lodge and bar were located, fishing camps were developed along the shoreline. Wealthy tourists would visit for a week, trying their luck at the elusive Beardslee. Years later, a road was cut to the lake's east end, and a steam ferry was launched. There was a photo of Joe's father on that ferry the first day it operated.

The south shore of the lake had four points of land, each projecting into the water. The road laced the south shoreline tightly, making hairpin turns on each point. I was to meet Joe on the first point past "Ambulance Bend." This curve was named after an accident thirty years prior where a loaded ambulance took the turn too quickly, lost control and plunged into the lake. The water depth drops off quickly in Lake Crescent. Legend has it that the ambulance shot out into the water and sank one hundred feet to the lake's bottom. While the driver survived, a logger in the rear, suffering from a lost limb, was secured to his gurney and drowned.

I pulled off the main road and onto the point, parked and walked through the trees to the end. As I cleared the grove of pines, I saw the lake's edge. Joe had his boat, a seventeen-foot Bayliner, drifting fifty feet offshore. The lake was calm. Joe didn't see me. I stood and watched him.

Joe was standing on the bow of his boat, wearing nothing but tattered denim cutoffs. For a man of his age, he was in very good physical shape. His skin sagged a bit around his waist and chest but did so minimally and only under the weight of the skin itself, not fat. Clearly, he had been a very thin, strong man in his younger years. He rubbed his face with one hand while slicking his hair back with the other. He dropped both to his sides, snapped the water off them twice, and wiggled his toes forward over the gunwale of the boat. He sprang forward off the bow and grabbed his knees midair, cannonballing into the cold water. When he surfaced, I clapped.

He looked startled as he realized he was being watched. When he saw me laughing, he grinned, his aged smile emerging from the surface of the water as he spoke.

"How high was my splash?" he asked.

"Ten feet!" I lied.

"Swim out here," he ordered. "Let's get goin'."

I jumped into the cold water, my breathing becoming erratic as it stunned my diaphragm. I swam out to the boat. As I climbed up the ladder in the stern, Joe grabbed my arm and pulled me in.

"Ya eat?" he asked.

"A little," I responded. "Why, you hungry?"

"Na, but I brought some of me cherries. Ya gotta have cherries when yer fishin'."

Joe reached behind him and pulled out a Styrofoam bowl full of fresh picked cherries, red as blood, with intact stems. "I also got you a cup," he stated. He pulled out two tin mugs, patiently pushing them slowly into the lake, allowing water to pour in from the sides. "Gotta drink water," Joe ordered. "The sun'll kill ya if ya don't drink water." Past a mouthful of sweet cherries, I mumbled, "Thanks."

We fished all morning, trolling forty yards of lead-weighted line. I sat in the stern next to the rods as Joe drove slowly. The sun was beating on my head and piercing my eyes; I pulled my hat down and leaned back. I was just dozing off to sleep when Joe screamed.

"Get 'em!" he ordered.

My head shot upright, flinging my hat onto the boat's deck. Joe pointed to one of the rods in the boat's holsters, doubled over and quivering with life. Joe scrambled to the console, feverishly threw the throttle into idle, and staggered to the back of the boat. He reached around me from behind, tightening the drag. The fish was stripping line despite the boat's lack of movement.

"Crank!" he screamed. "Show that fish who's boss."

I wound as quickly as I could, clear water spinning off the reel as its bail twirled. My forearms burned under the tension. Joe continued to coach me, bossing me in one ear, then twirling around my back and bossing into the other. He dashed about the boat, tossing rope and a gaff about in an attempt to free his net, which was sloppily pinned to the boat's upholstery with a rusty lure. He frantically ripped the net upward from the boat's wet fabric, slammed it into the water, and came up with the shiny creature. It was a gorgeous fish. Steel blue with a faint red stripe running its entire length.

"Beardslee?" I asked ignorantly.

"Yup," Joe replied. "A tiny one." He pulled out a splintered yardstick and laid the fish on top.

"Seventeen inches and as fat as can be," Joe proudly announced. "But they have to be twenty-one to keep."

I gently held the fish with both hands and slipped it into the lake, rocking it back and forth into the crisp water, aerating its gills. After a few moments, I released it. The fish threw out a few weak flips of its tail, turned belly-up, and floated to the surface. I dropped my head.

"Don't worry, kid. Happens. You'll catch another."

Joe started the engine, dropped two lines into the water, and drove off. I sat in the back, fixated on the silver flash on the water's surface shrinking as it was distanced from us.

"Eagle!" Joe shouted. I cocked my head backward and scanned the ridgeline of Pyramid Mountain to which Joe was pointing. The enormous bird coasted effortlessly toward the lake, its black body blending into the dark evergreens on the mountainside. Its stark white head twisted slightly to the side as it circled twice and shot downward toward the lake at a steep angle. Just prior to striking the surface of the lake, its glide leveled off. It lowered its claws from under its broad wingspan and scraped the surface of the water. A splash, a few flaps of its gigantic wings, and the eagle shot upward, my dead trout arcing in its sharp talons.

"I've only seen that twice before," Joe bragged. He spun around in his chair and continued to drive.

For the next few hours, we talked a lot. He told me about his family and how he was the only one of his six siblings still alive. He told me about the biggest fish he'd ever caught, which he claimed was "not much smaller than you, boy." The more interest I showed, the more spectacular the stories became. Mountain lion attacks, bear charges, and trees bigger than tractor trailers. Some were true I suppose, some could not possibly have been. Regardless, I sat quiet and entertained, not challenging even the most sensational tales, partially out of curiosity as to how grandiose the stories would become, but mostly out of respect. Abruptly, in the middle of a story about a herd of elk that used to swim across the lake twice per year, my rod buckled over.

I snapped up the rod, this time tightening the drag myself, having learned a lesson from Joe. I reeled for about fifteen minutes, brought the fish to the boat's side, and gave Joe a nod. Without a word, he smoothly netted the fish and laid it on the yardstick. The fish was even fatter and longer than the previous, its silver sides reflecting the sun's intense light into my squinting eyes. Joe adjusted the fish's tail to match the end of the yardstick. Its nose rested cleanly on the twenty inch mark. The trout, gasping for air, opened its mouth as it gave a mighty effort to wriggle out from under Joe's hand. He forcefully pinned the fish back onto the yardstick. Its nose now rested on the twenty-one inch mark.

"There's your Beardslee, boy. Twenty-one inches. A keepa. Saw it with me own eyes."

He handed me the fish, which I placed in the livewell. We reeled in the lines and drove full throttle back to the point near Ambulance Bend. He cut the engine as we approached, allowing the boat to drift toward the shoreline. I jumped off the bow onto the rocks; Joe sprang off the back of the boat into the water and waded around, fish in hand.

"Hold on, Joe. I have something for you." I ran to the car, retrieved a bottle of whiskey, and handed it to him.

"No thanks, kid. I only drink my screwdrivers. But don't worry none. The boys back at camp will empty 'er faster than you can skin a buck."

"I can't skin a buck, Joe," I retorted.

"Neither can I, kid!" he confessed as he laughed.

Joe pressed one finger against the outside of one nostril, cocked his head, and blew snot onto the ground. He lifted the same hand and offered it to me.

"Good day fishin', kid" he said as I cringed but shook his damp, sticky grip.

As I gathered my things and walked through the trees, I saw Joe climb back into his boat. I shuffled over exposed tree roots and under low pine branches back toward the car. Just before I lost sight of the lake, I looked back and gave Joe a wave. He was standing on the boat's gunwale. He waved. I turned my back toward the lake and heard a splash. I looked back. The boat rocked, empty, as a foamy ring settled in the water just off the stern.

The sun was setting, and after three hours of fishing the inlet to the lake, I had not seen a single rise. Despite the hatch, which I thought I had confidently matched, there was no activity on the water. My elbow grew sore from the repetitive presentation of various dry flies, all unproductive. I had exhausted all hope of catching a fish that night, so I initiated the same routine I do each time I prepare to end a session of fishing: allow myself five more casts. And one for good luck.

On the sixth cast, I began to retrieve line with my reel as I walked backward through the water toward the shore. Like a jolt of electricity, my rod tip came alive, gyrating and flexing to such a great degree that I feared it would break. Before I could react, or loosen my drag, I felt a snap, the gyration stopped, and the rod tip flipped upward, settling to a still posture in the air, limp line hanging from its top eyelet.

When I drove off the peninsula for the last time that summer, I passed the same waterfall I had seen each day and come to take for granted. I took pause at the fine mist that drifted from its plunge pool and the colorful spectrum it produced as it spritzed the road with moisture. I stopped to gas up the car a few miles down the road, browsing the local newspaper on the hood of the car as the archaic pump's numbers flipped over. I turned to the local news section. Crammed in the bottom corner was a small block of print entitled "Fishin' Report and Joe's Tips." It read, "Troll deep with ½ oz spoon or jig. Watch out for the heat. Make sure you and the boys drink plenty of water."

GRIZZLIES, TROUT, AND THE CITY OF BROTHERLY LOVE

TURTLE TAXI TYPICALLY doesn't provide service to White Ledge Campground. It's out of their range. However, the dispatcher with whom I spoke happened to be a patient of mine and sent out a wary driver to my New Hampshire home as a favor. Jeremy and Chris were too drunk to drive and needed a ride back to their tent at the campground. I'd intentionally not offered my backyard or guestroom as I knew the ruckus we'd raise over a campfire would wake my kids.

Jeremy took the bottle of scotch by its neck, braced his other hand on my shoulder for balance, and announced, "To Glacier." He pinned the vessel to his lips and emptied the remaining third of whisky into his mouth. His arm dropped as he shot me a glazed look. Then, as if clubbed in the head, he dropped from his standing position onto his face, out cold.

Turtle Taxi pulled up minutes later. Jeremy was breathing, not bleeding and seemed as if survival were probable; so Chris and I poured him into the taxi, reassuring the skeptical driver that the lump of a man we'd delivered was fine but reminding him to pull over if Jeremy started to vomit. I haven't seen or heard from Jeremy since.

Jeremy was an awkward guy with terrible asthma and a peculiar sense of humor that he attributed to his upbringing in a strict Jewish home and the influences of his eccentric parents, both math professors at the University of Illinois. He had untamed curly hair and a smooth face, which he proudly bragged never required shaving. He usually wore white sweatpants pulled up to his calves and old concert T-shirts, none more recent than REO Speedwagon's 1990 tour. He'd moved to Boston where he looked me up on the internet and invited himself to my house, ignoring my hints about being too busy and having a newborn baby. I'd met him years before while working in the bar and restaurant at Many Glacier Lodge in Montana's Glacier National Park.

We didn't have a lot in common. Jeremy was a collector of Phil Collins cassettes. I liked the Dave Matthews Band and Richard Shindell, a folk artist with the songwriting talent of Bob Dylan and the voice of Jim Croce. I enjoyed hiking. Jeremy liked rodeos but was afraid of ponies. Despite the incompatibility, I trolled him up as a backpacking partner for my last overnight fishing trip of the summer in Glacier. A coworker of mine had recently been consumed by three grizzlies hiking alone in the park, and although through the park's forensic work the bears were located and killed, I wanted company as I'd be camping. Jeremy said he was up for the trip if he could only find some shoes.

The dress code for waiters in the dining room in the lodge was strict. Black shoes. Tie. Slacks. I never saw Jeremy wearing anything other than his work shoes that summer; he lived in his dress shoes, which he often wore with his sweatpants, a fashion offense to which he was obtuse. Hours before our departure, he borrowed a pair of bright white Velcro diabetic shoes from one of the cooks. Available only by prescription, the kicks he sported were exceptionally padded and extra wide to prevent toe ulcers. They were size eleven. Jeremy wore a nine. The trip was saved.

We arrived at Avalanche Lake early in the afternoon. I'd read it held a healthy, native, naive population of cutthroat trout, just what my damaged ego needed after two fruitless days of fishing on nearby Otokomi Lake. Otokomi's fish were abundant and huge. Most over eighteen inches, the hungry creatures sucked hatching flies off the water's surface with the efficiency of a DustBuster. However, they'd not grown to be that large by falling for poorly tied patterns like those I winged at them. I had left empty-handed.

Avalanche Lake was a brilliant sapphire hue, which stood in stark contrast to the giant hemlocks along its shore. It sat at the end of a valley in a bowl-shaped mountain pocket that had been symmetrically scooped out by a glacier, now long gone. We camped on the western shore of the lake, a few minutes from the water's edge. Setting up the tent, I grew concerned with the gashes in the nearby trees, consistent with damage from razor-sharp bear claws. One tree had been worn smooth on one side, its bark missing. This finding was consistent with a bear's "rub" from back scratching. It was clearly fresh. There were grizz in the area.

Trees that lined the lake made backcasting impossible from anywhere other than the set of flotsam logs that had stacked up at the lake's outlet. I waded among the waterlogged timbers, peeled out a handful of bright yellow line, teetered on the logs, and managed to cast a #16 Adams, a common utilitarian fly pattern, onto the glassy surface of the water. In less than a second, it vanished in a turbulent swirl. My rod flexed. Gentle twitching on the end of my rod transmitted to my hand as I easily retrieved my line. I netted my catch, a six-inch golden cutthroat trout with ruby red gills and the prominent crimson throat for which it is named. I slipped it back into the water and recast my line. Again, the fly was sucked under the surface. I landed and released another cutthroat, same size, same vibrant colors.

Fishing Avalanche Lake. (Brian Irwin self-portrait.)

The bountiful pond continued to yield fish with each and every cast until my arm was tired. Jeremy had even taken the rod for a few throws and come up with fish. We quit and settled back into camp. The stove whispered as it cooked our noodles; we sat in silence, sipping whiskey. As the sun dipped behind the sharp ridge above our camp, it cast a sheet of light into the sky, outlining the contour of the rocky arête. Walking high above us, slowly and deliberately, was a grizzly, its silver-tipped hump as sharp as the barb on my tired Adams.

My family visited Glacier when I was a teenager. My father and I caught a few cutthroat the first day of that trip, and I immediately became impassioned by the idea of living and working in that untamed land. I didn't have the chance to pursue such an adventure until the summer following my first year of medical school. After driving from Pennsylvania, I showed up alone, dirty and poorly prepared, and asked for a job waiting tables at Many Glacier Lodge, the grandest in the park. I got it.

The hundred-year-old Many Glacier Lodge had a huge open lobby, five stories high. Lodgepole pines towered over the enormous, centrally located fireplace. Giant beams spanned the ceiling, inducing vertigo if viewed from below. The area around the lodge was frequented by grizzlies as well as black bears. It wasn't uncommon to have the hotel manager drop into the pub or restaurant and warn employees that a grizz had parked itself on the steps of the employee housing cabin, blocking entry. We all hiked with pepper spray. We screamed, "Whoa bear!" as we walked in the woods. Except for one bizarre waiter named Ned, who'd landed at Glacier after losing his life savings on the unsuccessful launch of a revolutionary new spatula he thought would reform the food service industry, no one hiked alone.

But fishing was another story. I preferred to fish alone, especially when fishing the reliable, feverous evening hatch on Swiftcurrent Lake. I often fished alone when I was upset, pensive, or morose. I still do. It's a habit I took on as a child. My father taught me to fly-fish on gentle Maryland streams when I was in second grade. The annual three-day fishing trips on which he took me are among my most treasured experiences. I tediously prepared my tackle so that it precisely matched my father's. My line clippers had to be on the same pocket of my fishing vest as his. My dry flies, streamers, and leaders had to be distributed into the same types of fly boxes and vest pockets as his. Even my vest itself had to match his: a homemade garment sewed by my mother out of my father's retired army shirts. He was issued two shirts during his service. From these, my mother crafted two vests.

I always wanted to fish right next to my father. I wanted him nearby so he could compliment my casting and be proud of me, should I ever land a trout, which for me took years. During the first trip with my father, I grew frustrated at the picky fat rainbow trout that refused to take my fly. I'd spooked him, which only made me madder at myself. Casting harder and more impatiently, I snagged a tree, fiercely shook my rod as I lost my temper and broke my rod. My dad drove us home, got me a new rod, and the trip continued. However, when we got back to the creek, I waded upstream, out of sight, and casted alone. For the rest of my life that's how I'd fish.

Each night, Swiftcurrent consistently boiled with rising brook trout, rarely more than eight inches long, just before sunset. The fish were emerald green, nearly as bright as the tiny brookies we'd pull from Maryland's miniscule boulder-choked streams of my youth. The fish were plentiful but lacked any selectivity at all, making the idyllic body of water the ideal place to not only falsely inflate my fishing ego but also provide escape from the hectic, loud, and unpleasant atmosphere of Philadelphia and medical school to which I'd return in the fall. Each night as I fished the lake, I grew sadder about having to leave Montana and return to the city where I was learning to become a doctor.

Incoming storm and rainbow over Swiftcurrent Lake as seen from Many Glacier Lodge, Glacier National Park, Montana. (Brian Irwin photo.)

I hated Philadelphia, and if I hadn't been pleased with the medical education I was getting, I would have perused transferring. I craved the open outdoors and felt suffocated in the city. Other than city parks, which to me seemed too tidy and contrived, it seemed there wasn't any escape from this initial year of med school. I had a crazy roommate who kept a jar of pickles next to his bed at all times. Once, the police shut down my road because a neighborhood kid unearthed a fractured human skull in his backyard. The closure happened again a week later when someone discovered a dead body in the Taco Bell dumpster. I had a friend and classmate fall into a canyon and die. I was feeling stressed from the competition, academic pressure, and the sadness of seeing people pass away for the first time in my life. I tried to find solace by fishing local waters, but the result was disappointing.

The dangers encountered in the wilds of Philly's waters were not bears. They were stray bullets or other city hazards of the like. The first time I fished the urban waters of Wissahickon Creek, a stabbing victim stumbled out of the bushes crying for help, forcing me to help him when I didn't even yet own a stethoscope. The second time I fished that stream, I tore my waders on a rusty, submerged, discarded bike, and I foul-hooked a dirty diaper from the streambed. I caught no fish.

The fish of Montana's clean waters were as bright and healthy as Philly's were thin and ridden with heavy metals. And although some of the alpine tarns held only growth-stunted trout, not all the fish around Many Glacier were miniature. Minutes east of the lodge sat the border of the Blackfeet Indian Reservation and the town of Browning. The impoverished village was one of the roughest settlements I'd seen since I'd left Philly. Walking down the street alone, I felt the same intuitive danger I'd learned to smell on uncomfortable evenings leaving hospitals or clinics in Philadelphia. In both the City of Brotherly Love and in Browning, I was the only "white man" strolling down the sidewalk, in the fly shop, or in the grocery store. In both places, I was pierced by stares as I stood in line at the store; comments about my short stature were shouted across the street to me as I briskly walked back to my car.

Substance abuse and violence were common issues in Browning. The front page of the daily paper—and years later, an episode of the television show *COPS*—vividly displayed Browning's problems.

Resentment and tension between the Native Americans and the "white men" are common in the region, an inevitable outcome of decades and decades of governmental policies that stripped our native people of their land and squeezed them into "reservations" with scant medical resources, marginal schooling, and the infrastructure that can support nothing more than a perennially hurting economy. Except for the local fishing guide services, most businesses in town were struggling and had been forever. I found it ironic that here, in the still ponds of the Rocky's eastern slope, huge native trout thrived, growing fat and long. While just down the street, the native people struggled to afford food for themselves or their children.

I was growing depressed with the reality that my summer was slipping away and that I was being slowly reeled back east. Certainly pulling a few trout from the still ponds of the plains on which the sad town sat would cheer me. The largest lake outside Browning sits in a depression. I had been warned by the local fly shop that steep banks drop to the water's edge where a ring of cattails line the pond's edge, making casting impossible from the shore. Although the overall vibe in town was unreceptive, the fly shop owner was pleasant and helpful when I told him of my plans to fish his local waters.

The tall man wore a black shirt that sported an airbrushed image of a wolf. His hair was jet black, shiny, and pulled taut into a ponytail. He tapped the pointed toe of a worn, ornately stitched cowboy boot as he pondered the answer to my questions about what fly patterns he preferred. He smiled widely, the woody knock of his boot against the tile floor tapping as he proudly disclosed how to get to his local secret spot which, although I was unable to confirm this, he claimed yielded the Montana state record brown trout.

He generously lent me a float tube, a sort of one-man inflatable fishing raft. I dragged it down to the lake's shore, clumsily climbing in and paddling my way into the middle of the lake. Beyond the bank at the end of the lake sat the snowcapped peaks of Glacier National Park, eased into an amber hue as the sun began to set. Just as the friendly shopkeeper promised, a caddis fly hatch exploded from the glassy surface of the lake.

I'd never fished from a float tube before. The unsteady gyration of the strange craft made casting awkward; however, the tube provided me with new artillery beyond my only other tools, which previously consisted of an average cast and a limited selection of flies. It provided me with the ability to quietly stalk ravenous trout by extending my cast and my body to them. Buoyant, surrounded by a big sky above and water all around, fishing from a float tube yields a unique sense of isolation and independence that can't be found in streams or rivers.

I peeled ten quick arm lengths of line off the reel, the buoyant cord coiling up in front of the tube. A few false casts later and I dropped my line and caddis pattern into the fading rings on the water's surface where seconds earlier a trout had risen. One slow retrieve and the fly vanished in a turbulent swirl of water, the paddle-shaped tail fin of a trophy-sized brown trout slapping the water as fly line evaporated from the coiled pile in my lap. I tightened the line with my fingers as the tube slowly crept forward in the water being slowly, but positively, dragged forward by the fighting fish. I eased the last of the slack line onto the rod, raised my arm to start what I was sure would be a long battle, and felt a pop. My tube eased to a halt. A long length of line floated on the water, straight as the needle on as compass, pointing directly into the setting sun.

My next few casts drew hungry fish to the surface of the smooth lake, and after a few hours and a few misses, I'd landed and released a half-dozen plump champagne-colored browns. Their hooked jaws and sharp teeth shredded my fly into an ugly collection of broken feathers and thread. As I pulled the tube from the water, I squinted in the dusky light. I scanned the horizon and the field that separated me from my car. I remembered the story on the second page of Browning's newspaper that I'd read in the fly shop earlier that day. The headline read, "Local Cattle Mauled by Grizzly, At Large."

At summer's end, I left Glacier, alone in the same dusty Honda Civic in which I'd arrived. As I drove down the valley, I stopped to have a last look at the turquoise lake and the wedge-shaped mountains that formed the backdrop, the now almost-extinct band of ice that is Grinnell Glacier, clinging to the cliff that formed the skyline. I gazed at the hillside behind my cabin where my friends had held a bonfire and good-bye party for me the night before. The charred remains of the fire stood out like a black scar on the green hillside. Around the fire pit circled a cinnamon-colored grizzly and two bear cubs.

Approaching Grinnell Glacier, Glacier National Park, Montana. (Brian Irwin photo.)

I was embarking on scenic, circuitous five-day drive back to the urban jungle of Philadelphia. On that trip, my inner monologue played back memories of a rich summer, eclectic friends, and rising fish to the background music of Richard Shindell. I slept in my car every night, sometimes in carwashes, sometimes at trailheads, after long days of driving and fishing. By the trip's end, I'd waded and angled the waters of the Snake River, the Yellowstone, the Blackfoot, and any of the great waters of the American West that were within my reach and pulled out and put back more trout, and even Arctic grayling, than I have in the eight cumulative years since.

The first night after I left Many Glacier, I drove until 3:00 a.m. Fueled by loud music and iced tea, I sped down the road that paralleled the Gallatin River, the trees poorly illuminated by the weak candlepower of a single headlight. The other one had been disabled by an unrepaired wiring problem that occurred in the beginning of the summer when I accidently drove over and eviscerated a corpulent marmot after it sprinted in front of my car.

I pulled off the highway onto an unmarked dirt road that leads toward the Gallatin. As I rounded the corner, my headlight revealed a concrete slab in a clearing on top of which sat an orange helicopter rigged with a giant bucket, the type used to dump water on forest fires. I parked off the slab, the blades of the chopper looming over my vehicle. I turned off my engine and allowed my pupils to stretch themselves open to welcome the light of a rising full moon and a myriad of stars. There was bear scat on the road adjacent to the helipad.

A short distance away was the edge of what is arguably the finest trout river in North America. I knew tomorrow I'd fish it and was excited, but exhausted. I hadn't talked to another human in days and was dreading the fall, when medical school would resume. I splashed crisp water on my face and sat down on a boulder at a sharp bend in the river. In the belly of the meander, the water flattened out. Its surface reflected the creamy glow of the moon. On top of the pool's water subtle rings silently opened, each one releasing a hatching insect into the warm night sky. With an energetic thrash, a fish tore through the smooth face of the river, leaving behind a few bubbles and ripples that radiated out and vanished, releasing the water to once again bounce the brilliant light of the moon and the stars into my tired eyes.

I watched the feeding pods of fish slurp insects as the dark water of the Gallatin slid by. I thought of the fast approaching morning when I'd drive out of Montana. Wondering if I'd ever return or if this wild place to which I ran could someday be my home, my mind heard the rich voice of Richard Shindell sing the story of a Mexican immigrant on the brink of deportation. "Senor, as you know I was a fisherman. How full the nets came in. We hauled them up by hand. But when we fled, we left them out by the coral reef. They're waiting there for me. Running deep."

Epilogue

The author on Pigeon Spire's *West Ridge*, Bugaboo Spires, British Columbia, Canada. (Paul Cormier photo.)

Strings

AN EIGHTEEN MONTH-OLD girl trips and falls head first into the dull corner of a woodstove in a cabin. The antiquated log camp sits on the shore of Daicy Pond in Maine's Great North Woods. The cut on her forehead doesn't bleed, but gapes open. The parents and their friend, the doctor, take the little girl to the local emergency room. He's sure the girl will need sutures. He's wrong. The emergency room doctor glues the wound shut, ensuring her future beauty. These parents have been his sounding board during his difficult divorce. They've pulled taut the strings of friendship, proving them to be strong. Like a marionette, he's been held up by those strings when he's least in balance.

The same doctor paddled a canoe around Daicy Pond later that evening. A mayfly hatch tested his fly-fishing skills. As he presented his flies to hungry, selective trout, some struck. When hooked they fought fiercely, stretching his fine monofilament string as he carefully dragged the fish into his boat. He always let the fish go, to live another day. Another fight. The finer the line the doctor chose to use, the more fish bit his imitations. And the more snapped his line, diving back deep into the dark water. To live.

Years before, a man arrived in the emergency room, breathing, but bleeding from his face. He'd put a gun into his mouth and fired a round into his head. The emergency room doctor in this small New Hampshire town, where the doctor practiced, called him from the adjacent room to help her. She used an old technique to establish an airway in this dying patient. Together, the doctor and the E.R. doctor threaded thick suture material into the skin on either side of the patient's throat. Applying counterpressure, these lines were pulled tight as a sharp, hollow, metal flange was plunged into the front of the patient's throat. It worked, meaning that a patent airway was established. But the patient was already too injured to survive. Like the sutures that went limp when the doctors released them, so did the patient's body as he slipped into death.

In 2008 two visionary Japanese climbers attempted to enchain two of Alaska's Kahiltna peaks with one of Mount McKinley's most challenging routes, the *Cassin Ridge*, something that had never been done before. The two vanished, leaving the climbing world wondering if they would ever be found, if they perished on the ascent, or if they "succeeded" and died on the descent. Over a year later, while looking for a different lost climber (who's never been found), a National Park Service helicopter spotted the deceased Japanese alpinists. They were still tied into either end of their rope. Unrecoverable due to altitude and location on the mountain, their bodies remain there today, frozen into the harsh mountainside.

The north face of Switzerland's Eiger, or "Norwand," is notorious for unpredictable rockfall and a litany of climbing accidents. The Norwand sits front and center to the tourist telescope on the deck of a nearby hotel in the idyllic village of Kleine Scheidegg. In 1957 catastrophe struck a four-man climbing party as they attempted the wall. Only one man was rescued. Two others fell to their deaths. The fourth was abandoned by rescue parties amidst a storm. He perished on the giant face. His corpse swung from his rope on the cliff for two years before it could be recovered, reminding gawking tourists of the gristly event.

While training in Colorado a young doctor attempted to climb *Stairway to Heaven*, a long ice climb near the town of Silverton, which sits at over 10,000 feet. Four ropelengths up, the naïve climber became exhausted in the thin air and difficult climbing conditions. Thirty feet above his belayer, who rested gingerly upon a weak, two-ice screw anchor, he lost grip of his ice tool and fell. He fully extended every inch of stretch in his rope and deployed a "screamer," a sewn device designed to absorb the energy generated by a falling climber. The anchor held. However the doctor landed on his belayer and their packs, clipped into the anchor by their nylon straps. The straps ripped under the pressure of the fall and launched into the canyon below. The stringy Achilles tendon in the doctor's left ankle ruptured during the accident. The pair spent hours evacuating back to their cars, the doctor hopping on one foot for many miles.

A little boy was born with a hole in the wall that separates the two main chambers of his heart. He struggled for weeks to gain weight, his lips becoming blue and his breath short with every feeding. Eventually his weight plateaued and the boy, just over eight pounds, was taken to the operating room. His heart was sliced open. The steady hands of his talented surgeon carefully sewed a synthetic patch over the hole and closed his chest with strong suture material. The knots of string in his heart now bear the force of squirting blood with each heartbeat, amounting to millions of beats over the now-healthy boy's existence. Those knots saved his life.

A forty-seven year old woman was born with a similar defect in her heart; a hole in the septum that separates the heart's two smaller chambers. She'd not undergone repair for many reasons, until one day she discussed it with her new doctor and was encouraged to have it fixed. In the same hospital as the little boy, she had her chest opened and her heart's hole sewn shut. She recovered in the same hospital unit as the little boy. Now her adult heart, strong and healthy, beats briskly without strain or difficulty. Those knots in her chest gave her hope.

A seventy year-old man left Canada to hike New Hampshire's Mount Washington. He left only scribbles in his journal as to his plan, discovered by authorities in his car after he was reported missing. An unsuccessful search was abandoned. A few weeks after his disappearance, when a hiker discovered his body coiled up like a snake under large boulders. The doctor was called, not in an attempt to save, but as part of a mass-dispatch that requested volunteers to help carry his remains up the mountain for evacuation. As the recovery party moved over lichen-coated boulders, breathing heavily through their mouths but not their noses, a cloudburst opened. The tight twang of the rescue litter's tensioned nylon straps rung out as they slipped over the knobby shoulders of the rescuers that carried its weight.

The damp air released warm drizzle onto the rocks and the recovery team, which inched slowly up the mountain. As the cadence of their uphill march beat, a brilliant rainbow evolved in the storm-darkened valley to their east, its ribbon of color glowing as brightly as the light of life.

GLOSSARY

aid climbing. A climbing technique whereby the climber uses (stands or pulls on) equipment that has been placed in the rock to gain upward progress, as opposed to using the rock's features to move upward.

Altiplano. The high altitude plains of Bolivia.

belayer. The person who controls the climbing rope in such a way that he or she "catches" the fall of their climbing partner.

belay device. A piece of climbing equipment that grips the rope, enabling a belayer to stop a fall, lower a climber, or rappel.

beta. A term that means information about a climbing or skiing route. Beta may include a route's description, its difficulty rating or details of its objective hazards.

bivy. Short for bivouac, to camp with minimal amenities, often on a climbing route.

bivy sack. A weatherproof fabric bag, similar to an uninsulated sleeping bag. in which a climber rests during a bivouac.

cam. A type of climbing protection, cams are spring-loaded units of climbing equipment designed to be inserted into cracks in rock and clipped to the rope.

couloir. A gully or slotlike weakness in a mountain's topography, which is often chosen as the line of ascent while mountain climbing or a line of descent while skiing.

cumulonimbus. A type of storm cloud, sometimes referred to as a thunderhead.

flake. A thin overlap of rock which is often gripped while climbing.

haul bag. A durable equipment bag designed to be pulled up a climbing route with ropes and, often, pulley systems.

jug. A relatively large, easily grasped protrusion of rock that is frequently gripped while climbing.

lenticular cloud. A form of cloud that often indicates high winds and foul weather. Shaped like a giant lens, these often form on the tips of mountains.

mantle. A climbing technique used to climb up and onto rocky ledges or a flat surface.

névé. Very firm snow, often formed from recurrent freeze-thaw cycles.

pin. Also known as a pitons, pins are iron or steel blades which are hammered into thin cracks in rock to be used as climbing protection (see below).

pitch. A section of a climbing route that is a natural stopping point. Typically a climber will climb one pitch, assemble an anchor, and then belay his or her partner as he or she climbs up to the anchor. The process is then repeated. Often a pitch is one full ropelength, but it may be shorter or longer depending on the availability of comfortable resting features on the climbing route.

protection. Equipment placed in rock or ice structures to which a climbing rope is clipped. Protection can be used to hold a climber in the event of a fall, build an anchor, or be used for upward progress while aid climbing.

rack. The assortment of protection carried on a climbing route.

rime. Frozen fog that collects on rocks, buildings, and other structures as a result of cold conditions and high winds.

screw (ice screw). A hollow screw, which can vary in length but is roughly one inch wide and at least a few inches long. These are screwed into the ice and used as protection while ice climbing.

serac. A block (usually quite large) of glacial ice that is formed by cracks, or crevasses, in the glacier's surface. Seracs often break free with little warning and may generate avalanches.

skins. Nylon or mohair strips that are applied to the bottoms of skis to enable a skier to glide uphill without slipping backward. These are then removed for the descent.

slackline. A long nylon strap strung taut between two immobile points. Slacklines are often walked like tightropes as a balance-improvement exercise.

step cutting. An early ice climbing technique in which small "steps" were chipped in the ice and used to ascend an icy climbing route.

tat. Old nylon cord or strapping left around trees or other features from previous climbing parties. These usually represent previous climbing anchors or points of protection.

triage. A system that screens patients in an attempt to prioritize them based on the severity of their conditions.

webbing. Nylon strapping used in climbing for multiple applications.

yurt. A portable wood-framed shelter used by nomadic peoples in Asia. These semipermanent structures are also used worldwide for recreation shelters (akin to a hut), homes, storage, and a multitude of other purposes.

ACKNOWLEDGMENTS

DEEPEST THANKS TO my friends for all their support and patience. Additionally, I owe appreciation to my little boys for providing me the rich experience of witnessing the wonders of the world through the lens of their innocent eyes. I would also like to recognize the efforts of the various individuals and editors with whom I've worked on some of these pieces, including Jeff Jackson, Alison Osius, Duane Raleigh, Craig Dostie, Peter Kray, George Hurley, and Katie Ives. You have all made the production of this book much easier. The New England Ski Museum, Rick Wilcox, Conrad Yager, Dave Lottman, Jay Mathers, and Brian Johnston generously contributed photos for which I am grateful. Lori Cashman should be recognized for her amazing understanding, backing, and devotion. Gratitude goes out to my sister Jessica for being my lifelong buddy. Likewise, I am forever indebted to my parents, Patricia and Robert, for their unwavering love and help through some of the most difficult times of my life. Finally, I want to extend additional thanks to my father, who taught me the value of the written word, offered the (sometimes unsolicited!) stroke of his red pen and taught me to take pride in my writing.

Breinigsville, PA USA
17 December 2009
229404BV00003B/4/P